Emotionally ENGAGED

Emotionally ENGAGED

A Bride's Guide to Surviving the
"Happiest" Time of Her Life

ALLISON MOIR-SMITH, MA

FOUNDER, EMOTIONALLY ENGAGED
COUNSELING FOR BRIDES

HUDSON
STREET
PRESS

HUDSON STREET PRESS
Published by Penguin Group
Penguin Group (USA) Inc., 375 Hudson Street, New York, New York 10014, U.S.A.
Penguin Group (Canada), 90 Eglinton Avenue East, Suite 700, Toronto, Canada M4P
2Y3 (a division of Pearson Penguin Canada Inc.)
Penguin Books Ltd, 80 Strand, London WC2R 0RL, England
Penguin Ireland, 25 St. Stephen's Green, Dublin 2, Ireland
(a division of Penguin Books, Ltd.)
Penguin Group (Australia), 250 Camberwell Road, Camberwell, Victoria 3124,
Australia (a division of Pearson Australia Group Pty. Ltd.)
Penguin Books India Pvt. Ltd., 11 Community Centre, Panchsheel Park,
New Delhi – 110 017, India
Penguin Books (NZ), cnr Airborne and Rosedale Roads, Albany, Auckland 1310,
New Zealand (a division of Pearson New Zealand Ltd.)
Penguin Books (South Africa) (Pty.) Ltd., 24 Sturdee Avenue, Rosebank, Johannesburg
2196, South Africa

Penguin Books Ltd., Registered Offices: 80 Strand, London WC2R 0RL, England

First published by Hudson Street Press, a member of Penguin Group (USA) Inc.

First Printing, February 2006
10 9 8 7 6 5 4 3 2 1

REGISTERED TRADEMARK — MARCA REGISTRADA

HUDSON
STREET
PRESS

LIBRARY OF CONGRESS CATALOGING-IN-PUBLICATION DATA

Moir-Smith, Allison.
    Emotionally engaged : a bride's guide to surviving the "happiest" time of her life /
Allison Moir-Smith.
        p.   cm.
    Includes bibliographical references.
    ISBN 1-59463-014-3 (alk. paper)
    1. Weddings — Psychological aspects.   2. Brides — Psychology.   I. Title.
    HQ745.M659   2006
    395.2'2 — dc22

                                                                        2005023960

Printed in the United States of America
Set in Cochin

For Jason

CONTENTS

Contents

Stage Three. Beginning

CHAPTER 1

The Happiest Time of My Life?
Yeah, Right.

It all started off happily enough.

In fact, I'm embarrassed to admit that I was an [Insert Groom] bride-to-be. You know the type: the single woman who secretly fantasizes about her wedding in such detail that when she finally meets Mr. Right and he proposes, planning the wedding is a snap. From the moment Jason popped the question, my secret wedding fantasy was unleashed.

I could picture it well: in eleven months' time, 120 guests would witness our marriage ceremony, held in a field on my parents' property beside the Connecticut River in New Hampshire. My maid of honor and two flower girls would be wearing sunny, canary yellow dresses, with daisies tucked behind their ears. Jason would wear a bright yellow tie to match. We'd toast with champagne in my mother's garden in its full summer glory and have dinner and dancing under a big white tent in the backyard.

My vision of our wedding was so complete that just two weeks after Jason proposed, I'd booked all the big-ticket items—the caterer, the tent, the DJ, and the Port-O-Potties

(a nasty necessity for a home wedding like ours). I'd even se-
cured the services of a wedding coordinator to ensure smooth
sailing. All I had to do for the rest of our engagement, I figured, was register for gifts (fun with a scanning gun!), be
feted by friends (kitchen shower, or bath?), worry about the
weather (I hope it doesn't rain!), and, of course, revel in how
lucky I was to be marrying the love of my life. I'd kissed a lot
of frogs during my eleven years in Manhattan, so I knew how
right our relationship was for me.

For two years, Jason and I sat side by side in graduate
school. As we worked toward our master's degrees in counseling psychology, our friendship deepened, slowly but surely.
Over time, this handsome, smart man with a big, compassionate heart became one of my closest friends. During the final
week of classes, our friendship bloomed into love. A year later
we were engaged, and I had that perfect foundation for a relationship that had always seemed so elusive when I was going on blind dates: I was marrying my best friend.

With Jason, I felt more natural, beautiful, and myself than
I ever had before in a relationship. I felt appreciated and accepted, supported and safe. (He even found my wedding fantasies endearing.) I loved, trusted, and admired him far more
than any other man I'd known. We both felt an enormous
amount of promise and hope about our married life together,
and we were grateful to have found each other.

So you can imagine that when, a few weeks after Jason
proposed, I started to feel sad, anxious, and irritable for days
at a time, I was confused, to say the least. One minute I'd be

giddily looking through books of invitations, the next I'd be lost in thought, reminiscing about some long-ago family vacation, nearly brought to tears by the memory. And at times, I became a complete bridezilla—a bitchy, self-absorbed, entitled, wedding-obsessed, perfectionistic, stressed-out nightmare of a person. (Which, I promise, is completely out of character.) There were days when, if a vendor didn't return my phone call within twenty-four hours, I'd go ballistic. If I missed a date on my to-do list, I'd panic that the whole schedule was out of whack. If someone offered a simple suggestion about our wedding, I'd be offended.

As the weeks wore on, I began to feel a deep pit of sadness in my stomach about leaving my single life, which baffled me because I was happy (and relieved) to have finally found my mate. At other times I felt paralyzed by fear of the future, even though being married to Jason was exactly what I wanted. When I talked to certain family members and friends about the wedding, I felt overwrought with guilt, like I was abandoning them by going off and getting married.

What I was feeling just didn't make sense; the contradictory emotions did not compute. *What the hell was going on with me?*

By the time the six-month countdown to our wedding began, the giddy and productive [Insert Groom] bride had completely vanished, and I sank into a dark, sad hole. Insomnia haunted me. Late at night I'd roam the apartment, worrying that I'd be a depressed bride. I envisioned myself walking listlessly down the aisle, indifferent to my husband-to-be and assembled guests. In those middle-of-the-night hours, I felt isolated and alone, cut off and unsupported by my family and friends, none of whom seemed to understand what I was feeling. When I tried to explain myself to them, they stared back at me quizzically, unable to fathom why I was upset when I *should* be so happy.

Worst of all, the emotional roller coaster I was on scared me. "Oh my God," I thought to myself. "If I'm feeling this upset all the time, does it mean I should call off the wedding?"

Then my mother and I started talking about lasagna, and everything fell apart.

The menu Jason and I had created for our casual rehearsal-dinner picnic beside a pond was supposed to be simple and fun. We thought that lasagna, Kentucky Fried Chicken, salads, beer, wine, and Klondike bars for dessert would be a nice contrast to the fancier sit-down wedding reception the following day.

Planning it, however, became a mother-daughter wrestling match. I was thirty-four years old, but I felt like a teenager again. My emotions were on full blast, as they'd been in high school, and again, I felt like I was on the losing side of a power struggle with my mom. The conversations between us went something like this:

MOM: How do you plan on keeping the lasagna warm?
ME: It'll be hot when the caterers deliver it.

MOM (one week later): How do you know it will be delivered hot?
ME: Because it's their job.

MOM (three weeks later): Why don't you keep them in the ovens at the club during cocktails?

ME: Okay, Mom. Good idea.

MOM (a week after that): I don't think the ovens are big enough. How do you *know* the ovens are big enough?

ME: I'll ask.

MOM (two weeks later): I'm still worried about the lasagna being hot.

ME: Oh my God, Mom! Okay, we'll rent chafing dishes.

MOM (the next day): Do you really think chafing dishes will work?

ME: Good Lord, Mom, *yes!* And if they don't, we'll have it lukewarm, because we don't care that much.

MOM (two weeks later): You know, lukewarm lasagna isn't very pleasant.

Each time we spoke on the phone, Mom mentioned the lasagna. No solution I offered allayed her worries. She talked to my dad about it ("I don't know how Allison's going to keep the lasagna hot"); to my two brothers ("I'm worried about the lasagna"); and to my four sisters ("Lukewarm lasagna isn't very nice, don't you agree?"). Even Cookie, her cleaning lady, got an earful ("Allison's having lasagna delivered to the rehearsal dinner"), as did anyone else who'd listen. My mother was driving me crazy, driving them crazy, and yet she could not be stopped. Or shut up.

In the eye of the lasagna storm and in a highly emotional state, I couldn't find my way out. For a good four months, the conversation went around and around like this before I realized that

(a) nothing I said or did would stop her lasagna obsession, and

(b) my mom and I weren't actually fighting about the temperature of the lasagna.

What were we fighting about? I didn't quite know yet — although I had an inkling that we were clashing about the changing nature of our relationship, as Jason and I prepared to marry. What I did know was that it was my job to figure out what was going on. Mom couldn't help; she was too busy worrying about the lasagna.

I smartened up and stepped out of the fight, even going so far as to hold the telephone away from my ear when the word "lasagna" crossed her lips. Instead of doing backflips for my mother, I became more of an amused spectator, keeping her craziness and her grievances at arm's length.

I decided to refocus my mental energy on the only person I had any control over: me. I knew that if I could make meaning of my sadness, anxiety, and fear, I'd be able to grow from what I was feeling, rather than just be battered by it. So I began to try to figure out what was going on with me and to learn from this crazy emotional world I had entered as a bride-to-be. Cold lasagna be damned.

Understanding My Craziness

The rare times I admitted to my conflicting emotions, I generally heard one pat response: "It's a rite of passage," family and friends would say. "Of course you're having a hard time." Rite of passage, rite of passage—I kept hearing the phrase over and over again.

"What the hell is a rite of passage?" I thought. "And why is it so damn hard for me?"

I'd just completed my master's degree in counseling psychology, so I knew the value of self-analysis—of closely observing and examining one's inner dialogue, thoughts, and behaviors. My hope was that by asking and answering the tough question—*Why, during the happiest time of my life, do I feel so bad?*—I would make sense of this strange experience. In other words, if I studied my emotions during my engagement, I'd know that all the angst I was going through wasn't for naught.

So I took myself on as a client and a research subject, so to speak. With my therapist hat on, I worked to understand my inner experience. Instead of fighting my feelings or trying to distract myself with the wedding to-do list, I became curious about my emotions. My inner dialogue—aka the whining in my head—changed from, "Why do I feel so bad all the time?" to "What can these 'bad' feelings tell me about myself?" I wrote pages and pages in my journal, and I continued to work hard in my weekly sessions with Ceil, my therapist, to be as self-aware as possible.

It took me a while to overcome the shame of not being a 100 percent happy bride. (Flipping through *Martha Stewart Weddings*, all the brides beamed big toothy grins at me. They seemed happy. And from what I knew, my married friends hadn't melted down the way I was; they seemed happy, too.) When I gave up that self-imposed struggle, however, I was able to look at how I was *really* feeling: happy, but also sad, scared, afraid, disappointed, ashamed, guilty, delighted, overwhelmed, confused—what a complex cocktail of emotions was roiling within me! No wonder I tried to keep the feelings at bay. Now, however, I was going to unleash them.

What happened? The anxiety, fear, and overwhelm quickly dissipated, and I was left adrift in a deep sea of sadness. Grief, even. It really felt like a death, a funeral of sorts, and though it didn't make sense at the time, I trusted it. I knew from my experiences both as a client in therapy and as a trained therapist that the only way out was through: I needed to *feel* my sadness before I could understand it. Then and only then would the grief truly pass, and I would feel fully happy again.

In an effort to make sense of my sadness, I went to the library and devoured whatever texts I thought might be helpful. My first order of business was to get to the bottom of this rite-of-passage business. What was a rite of passage, exactly, and how could I learn to go through mine more gracefully?

A rite of passage, I learned, is a ritual that helps a person pass from one life stage to another. Throughout our lives, we go through many rites of passage—birth, childhood, adolescence, adulthood, motherhood, the empty nest, old age, and death. Each passage is, essentially, a change of identity. We mark and celebrate these changes in identity with rituals: first communions, bat mitzvahs, sweet sixteens, baby showers, even funerals. The purpose of these events is to help us pass from one defined position to another, to facilitate the separation from an old identity and the transition into a new one.

A wedding is the quintessential example of a rite of passage. (Turns out my family and friends were right!) To marry, the bride and groom leave their single lives and families of origin in order to begin their married life together as one new family. Traditional wedding rituals encourage this separation. The single girlfriends throw a last-hurrah bachelorette party before the bride goes off into marriage. The bride wears different clothing than her bridesmaids, signaling her separation from them. The father gives the daughter away to her husband-to-be at the altar. When viewed through this rite-of-passage lens, a wedding's ingrained traditions, its universal structure, and even its insanely detailed planning process help women make this break with their former realities.

Learning this helped a bit, but I was still confused. Why was I so sad and scared when I was doing exactly what I wanted to do—get married to Jason? Because, I learned, I was going through a major life transition. Neither single nor married, during my engagement I was in the process of leaving my single life (without having fully left it) and, at the same time, entering married life (without being fully a part of it). No wonder I was such a wreck.

That I was grieving the end of my single life was a counterintuitive, unconventional, and revolutionary way to think about being engaged. It debunked the myth that this was the happiest time of my life. And that gave me freedom to do the psychological work I needed to do before I walked down that aisle.

There are many layers to leaving single life, I discovered. During my engagement, as I made Jason and our marriage-to-be number one in my life, I noticed how that impacted all my other relationships. To some degree, every single relationship I had was changing in ways I had never anticipated now that my relationship with Jason was becoming my top priority.

My relationship to myself as a single woman. As a single person, I'd focused on *my* career, *my* social life, *my* needs, and *my* life, and I'd accomplished and learned so much: how to be an adult, to live on my own, and to rely on myself. In getting married, that era was over. I was moving away from a life of solitude to a life of interdependence. While I was relieved to leave dating behind for good, and happy and hopeful about our future, the strongest emotions I had were nostalgia for my single days and anxiety (Who am I now?). My essential self—my personality, independent spirit, heart, and soul—remained the same, of course. But the part of me that was a single woman was in flux.

My relationship with my family. As the new Jason-and-Allison family started to become number one in my life, my parents and siblings dropped down a notch. After thirty-four years of devoting all my familial energy to them, now I was directing that energy to Jason. After more than three decades of my family identity being "daughter," now I was becoming "wife." I was loosening my emotional and psychological ties to my family so that I could form a deeper bond with Jason; I was leaving my family, breaking away from them — rejecting them, in a sense — choosing Jason. Butting heads over the lasagna was actually helping me to do it. Still, leaving my parents' family and letting go of my primary family identification as their daughter was grueling.

My relationships with my single girlfriends. I was entering a life — married life — my single girlfriends didn't and couldn't know. I had essentially abandoned "the girls," since now most of my energy went to Jason. That made me feel guilty, scared, and sad because I missed the intense closeness and intimacy of our friendships. I knew that in some ways our friendships would never be quite the same now that I was about to have a husband. It was another major end of an era that I had to face.

My relationship with Jason. Now that we were getting married, our relationship took on a new seriousness. Our bond deepened, and we became even closer than we'd been as boyfriend and girlfriend, but at times we also struggled with each other a little more, clashing about personality differences, money, families, and day-to-day life. The life and relationship we were building together were strong and healthy, but I sometimes missed the lighthearted dating days, when it was all about having fun and being in love.

For the months of February, March, and April before our July wedding, I let go of my firm grip on the to-do list. I put aside the flowers and favors and went inward, into the sadness and fear I'd been avoiding. In this exploration, I reflected on all that I had accomplished and learned about myself during my single years. I evaluated my close relationships with family and friends, assessing the roles I'd played in my life thus far. I brainstormed about what I wanted to change about my relationships and what I wanted to keep. I sat in the uncomfortable anxiety about the changes my impending marriage would inevitably bring about in my relationships. I grieved the many endings in my life. In essence, I took stock of where I'd been the preceding thirty-four years and imagined where I wanted to go.

It paid off. Six weeks before our wedding, the gray clouds of grief lifted, and I felt genuinely happy and ready to get married. My worries about being a listless, depressed bride vanished because I was eager and ready to begin my new life with Jason. I had let go of my single girl–ness, and I felt more womanly, stronger, and more feminine than I ever had. After all my inner exploration, I felt more fully adult than ever before. I felt powerful and alive in a new and exciting way.

My goal for our wedding day was to feel all my emotions, to be emotionally present and not be so overwhelmed, nervous, or checked out that I'd have to watch our wedding

on video after our honeymoon. I wanted to experience whatever came up, be it full-bodied joy, big-time jitters, heart-
beating-fast fear, or wrenching sorrow. "Let 'em rip!" was my
private motto.

As the hairdresser pinned the family veil my four older sisters had all worn at their weddings into my hair, I cried as I
saw a bride—me!—in the mirror. Tears trickled down my
face as I realized the profundity of the next few hours. I cried
with sadness because I was now, literally, leaving the life I'd
known; with fear as I entered into married life, a state I knew
nothing about firsthand; and with complete joy that today
was the day I was finally marrying Jason. Emotions coursed
through me: I got my wish.

A few hours later, as my dad and I started making our way
down the meandering path to the ceremony, I asked him,
"How are you doing?"

He patted my arm, causing my bouquet of wildflowers to
shake. "Well, I'm happy to be gaining a son," he said glumly,
"but I'm sad I'm losing you."

"You know what, Dad?" I said. "That's exactly how I've
been feeling all year long—happy *and* sad." And we walked,
in a state of happy-sadness, down the path to where Jason
stood waiting for me with tears in his eyes.

Seeing Jason before me, my happy-sadness moved into
giddy excitement, then transformed into a calm, deep peace
during the ceremony, and finally turned into exultant and absolute joy during the recessional as Jason and I walked,
hugged, kissed, laughed, and stumbled into each other back
down the path as husband and wife. Our entire wedding day

was like that, a wave of one intense emotion after another. But in contrast to my engagement, on that day, I wanted to be on this emotional roller coaster. I wanted to feel every feeling so that I could witness myself manifest the inner identity shift from single to married woman, to gather the fruits of my emotional labor. And I did, big time.

At our wedding, sadness and fear were not uninvited guests. They were guests of honor because by working through them, I had transformed my engagement from a time of high stress to a time of self-discovery.

More Than Two Million Brides

During my engagement I learned how to turn my conflicting emotions into important personal growth. I wanted to help other brides-to-be do the same. So a few months after our wedding, I founded Emotionally Engaged Counseling for Brides and focused my psychotherapy practice solely on brides-to-be. I took a chance, thinking that if I felt that discombobulated during my engagement, some of the 2.3 million American brides who marry each year must feel the same way. Either that or I was one in 2.3 million and a complete freak.

Turns out I wasn't a freak at all. Within months, Boston brides-to-be were attending my workshops on Cold Feet, Becoming a We, and How *Not* to Be a Bridezilla on Your Wedding Day. The Saturday sessions began with overwhelmed brides-to-be walking into the room feeling stressed out and upset (some literally in tears). Four hours later, they walked out feeling calm, armed with the information and confidence to handle whatever emotions might arise.

Most brides attended the workshops hoping to learn how to eliminate their negative feelings. They were afraid to give in to their sadness and fear, thinking that once they turned on the faucet, they'd never be able to shut it off. In reality, emotions work the opposite way. When strong emotions are *not* felt, they grow in power and intensity; when they *are* felt, the sadness and fear pass through your system. Facing and feeling negative emotions can have a cathartic effect. It cleans house of the fear and sadness, doubt and worry, and makes room once again for positive feelings of joy, excitement, and happiness.

Workshop after workshop, I saw how empowering it was for brides to learn the benefits of connecting to their feelings and of understanding the psychological process they were going through as they prepared to marry. When they began to view their engagement as a time of self-exploration and discovery, their negative emotions became bearable. Welcome, almost. When brides-to-be could attach meaning and purpose to their angst, they once again felt in control.

Since 2002, thousands of brides from all over the world have found my Web site by Googling "cold feet," "engagement anxiety," or "sad bride." Often, they'll drop me an e-mail just to say, "It's good to know that what I'm feeling is completely normal." Or they'll call me up in disbelief that someone specializes in counseling brides, relieved that I can help them sort through their feelings. Over the last four years, I've counseled hundreds of brides over the telephone from New York to

California, Toronto to Tennessee. (Every March and April my phone rings off the hook, and traffic on my Web site triples. As spring and summer brides-to-be prepare to address the invitations, their stress levels skyrocket.) Even long-distance, I can hear brides-to-be sigh with relief when (a) they discover how normal they are, and (b) they understand that experiencing difficult emotions is necessary for them to reconnect to joy.

Bride-to-be Rachel,* whose story you'll get to know well, did just that. The twenty-seven-year-old financial analyst attended one of my workshops just weeks after she got engaged. That day, this tall, beautiful young woman looked drawn and exhausted, with dark circles of sleeplessness under her eyes, revealing how distraught she felt on the inside. In the workshop, she shared her troubles—how she had pushed her boyfriend to propose, yet now that she had that ring on her left hand, she didn't want to spread the word that they were engaged. She was scared this meant that she was making a huge mistake in marrying him.

"I'm a mess!" she said, tears welling up in her blue eyes. "I've wanted to be engaged for a long time, and now that I'm here, all I feel is scared—scared of getting married, scared of walking down the aisle with my dad, scared of moving out of my apartment. My wedding's not for a year. I'm not sure I can take a year of feeling like this."

Another bride-to-be in the workshop passed Rachel the box of tissues, and we all got down to work. We discussed

---

*All names and identities have been changed, and some of the brides-to-be in this book are composite characters.

what emotions naturally arise during engagement, why, and how to work through them; how to deal with the changing relationships with family and friends; what to expect in the weeks and months leading up to the wedding, the honeymoon, and the first year of marriage; and more. Through these discussions and by doing therapeutic exercises I designed specifically for brides-to-be, Rachel came to understand that her fears served a purpose beyond purely torturing her—and knowing this helped her deal with them.

Shortly after her wedding, Rachel sent me some photos of the happy couple. In one year's time, she had transformed from a terrified, sleepless bride-to-be to a beaming, beautiful, joyful bride.

Rachel was able to work through her cold feet and grow in the process. (You'll see how in the chapter titled "A Family Affair.") You can too. In this book, I've expanded the principles and techniques brides learn in my bridal workshops and individual counseling sessions.

All the brides I work with find it invaluable to learn about the three stages of getting married, a theory based on a rite of passage I've developed to describe the psychological process every woman goes through as she makes the change in identity from single to married. I call this process EBB—Ending, Bridging, and Beginning—and it forms the backbone of this book. EBB is an emotional road map to your engagement. When you know what stage you're in, you'll be able to plot your emotional path. You'll discover what's normal to feel at every stage and know what to expect, emotionally, in the months to come.

In this book, you'll read the stories of brides-to-be just like you. Most are based on the experiences of clients with whom I've worked individually or who have participated in my workshops. Others are composites of the more than twenty-five brides-to-be and newlyweds I interviewed for this book. Some you'll get to know quite well, including

- Cynthia, who worked through a bad case of cold feet that started just seconds after her fiancé proposed, and whose struggles with giving up her single identity persisted several months into her engagement.

- Sarah, who learned how to add the role of "wife" to her identity—an identity that was previously based almost exclusively on her career.

- And Carrie, who learned how to be in an intimate, trusting, lifelong committed relationship during her engagement, but only after a few frightening knock-down and drag-out arguments with her fiancé.

The brides-to-be depicted in this book share personal stories about their engagements that don't necessarily paint the prettiest or most pulled-together portraits. But the stories are real. In fact, some women asked to participate in this book because they wanted to spare future brides-to-be some of the disorienting loneliness they experienced during their engagements. They wanted to throw future brides-to-be a lifeline, in effect. So go ahead and grab hold.

To help you work through your complex emotions, in each

chapter you'll find some therapeutic exercises. I call them The Emotional To-Do List, and the items on this list are just as important as the items you check off your master wedding list—if not more so. (The Emotional To-Do List will relax and center you, while the daunting wedding to-do list will probably stress you out!) Created for my bridal workshops and tested by brides-to-be just like you, the exercises in The Emotional To-Do List will help you get to the heart of the emotional challenges you're experiencing.

You may want to keep a journal by your side as you read this book, not only to complete The Emotional To-Do List exercises, but also to write down your reflections as they come to you. As you read the stories of the brides-to-be, you're bound to gain important insights about your own specific situation. Jot down your thoughts in your journal, and keep it with you during your engagement.

You'll also get tidbits of advice from newlyweds who've made the transition from single to married and lived to tell the tale. Now, they're sharing their words of wisdom with you throughout the book in the "If I Knew *Then* What I Know *Now* . . ." boxes.

Finally, if you're worried that the cold feet you're experiencing might really indicate that you shouldn't in fact marry your fiancé, you can put your feelings to the test in the "Cold Feet Alert" boxes and exercises that appear at the end of chapters 2 through 6.

In planning your wedding, you're constantly making decisions. Should we serve chicken or beef? What looks better with my skin tone, ivory or white? Here's one more important decision to make: either you can ignore your inner turmoil, slap on a happy-bride smile, and write off all your "crazy" feelings to wedding-planning stress, or you can be aware of your inner emotional experience and transform your engagement into a time of self-discovery and personal growth.

This book is for brides-to-be who want to learn from the "crazy" emotions, not just be at their whim.

CHAPTER 2

The Fantasy vs. the Reality of Being Engaged
Wedding Myths Debunked

On her way home from work, Erica, a twenty-seven-year-old bride-to-be, stopped by the newsstand to pick up a stack of bridal magazines. Her agenda for the evening: a hot bath, a glass of wine, and the latest issue of *Bride's*. Heaven.

Flipping past ads for wedding gowns, crystal goblets, and sunny honeymoon destinations, Erica felt calm and content. Life was sweet.

Dan had proposed to Erica two months earlier, after three years of dating. They had been hiking through the Muir Woods in northern California when Dan dropped to one knee at the base of a giant primordial redwood tree. Erica's answer was an immediate, enthusiastic, and wholehearted "Yes!" They spent the rest of their vacation cocooning themselves, savoring their exciting secret.

Announcing their engagement after they returned from their trip turned out to be a blast. Both sets of parents were thrilled by the news, and they arranged the first Meeting Of The In-Laws for the following weekend. The family lunch couldn't have gone better; the dads talked shop and golf while the moms traded leads for florists and caterers for the wedding. Dan and Erica's friends threw a festive engagement party a few weeks later to celebrate. Everybody was heartened by their happy news and nuptials — especially Erica and Dan. They were giddy about their wedding, and looking forward to their future together.

They'd already been through a lot as a couple. They'd faced health crises, career challenges, and the loneliness of long-distance dating, and they knew they were a great team about to embark on an exciting life together.

Finished with *Bride's*, Erica hefted another five-pound bridal magazine onto her lap. As pages of smiling, picture-perfect brides slipped through her hands, she noticed a feeling of anxiety starting to rise within her. This feeling had become familiar to her over the past few weeks. Dress, cake, flowers, location, color scheme, food, favors, transportation, hotel reservations — just thinking about all the decisions they had to make made her heart race and her palms sweat. And yet, Erica sensed that it wasn't just the wedding that was making her upset.

Despite how excited she was to be marrying Dan, Erica felt as if her life had been turned upside down in the two months she had been engaged. As well-behaved as her parents were at the in-laws lunch, they were driving her crazy. They insisted that the wedding be a formal, black-tie affair (and since they were picking up the tab, their influence couldn't be blown off), while she and Dan wanted something much more casual — a barbeque or a luau — that reflected who they were as a couple. Then there were the problems with her girlfriends. After the engagement party, it felt as if they had all but abandoned her, disappearing into their girls-about-town single lives. They called her to go out for drinks less often, and her pals had stopped dissecting the daily trials and tribulations of their single lives with her. Something was going on between her and Dan, too. After three peaceful, nonconfrontational years of dating, they were bickering like cats and dogs about everything, from how to squeeze the stupid toothpaste tube to how often they were (or were not) having sex. And, on top of everything, Erica found herself in the throes of a full-on identity crisis. "Me?" she thought. "A wife? But I'm only twenty-seven. How can I be a wife . . . *like my mom*?" Erica had hoped that looking through the bridal magazines would calm her nerves and reignite her giddy excitement about her wedding. Alas, that plan backfired, and she felt more stirred up than ever.

Erica tried talking about her anxiety to close friends and family, but she was met with blank stares. Or they quickly steered the conversation to the wedding, quizzing her about her dress (no, she hadn't found one yet), the honeymoon (Aruba or Mexico, they were still deciding), and the menu (tense negotiations with her parents over filet mignon vs. sea bass were still in progress). Feeling the pressure to be a happy bride coming at her from all directions, Erica drove her upset emotions underground and plastered a smile on her face. "Yes, I am *so* excited about getting married!" she responded through gritted teeth.

Emotionally, being engaged was much more complicated than the sweet fairy tale Erica had always imagined it would be. Her entire life, whenever Erica had envisioned her engagement, she had expected it to be a time of closeness with her parents (not squabbles over sea bass), last hurrahs on the town with her single girlfriends (not total abandonment by them), and romance with her fiancé (not the petty arguments they seemed to be having). So she took to the Internet to figure out why she was feeling both happy and anxious at the same time. After finding my Web site, she called me up. "One minute I'm excited about getting married, the next I'm crying," Erica said to me.

I'd heard stories similar to Erica's hundreds of times before, and as a bridal counselor, I knew that what she was going through was perfectly normal. Part of what was making Erica miserable was that she was wedded to her fairy-tale idea of being engaged. Like many brides-to-be, Erica was clinging to the myths that her parents would be perfect, her friends by her side, and her fiancé goo-goo-eyed at all times. When her reality as a bride-to-be didn't live up to her image of perfection, she thought something might be horribly wrong—with her, with him, with the marriage, with what she didn't quite know. What she did know was that the gulf between her fantasies and her realities as a bride-to-be sometimes made her feel a little crazy and more than a little upset.

"So I'm not abnormal?" Erica asked.

"Not at all," I replied.

Let's take a look at some of those insidious myths that make brides-to-be feel so crazy. In fact, let's debunk them.

Fantasy: *Your engagement will be the happiest time of your life.*

Reality: Your engagement will actually be one of the most up-and-down times of your life; your *wedding day* will be one of the happiest *days* of your life.

Why? Planning one of today's elaborate weddings can drive even the most organized type A bride-to-be to pull her hair out. But it's a piece of cake compared to the psychological changes a woman undergoes before she gets married.

Most brides-to-be write off their "unbridely" feelings of anxiety, fear, and sadness to wedding stress. However, while wedding stress does in fact account for some of the angst, much of it is caused by a normal, natural psychological process that every woman goes through as she prepares to marry.

From the moment you say yes to the popped question, you are tossed into limbo, an unknown, in-between, new world in which you're neither single nor married, neither girlfriend nor wife. Your sense of who you are suddenly feels shaky as you close the chapter on your single life and begin a new one as a married woman.

Your relationships are changing as a result of your engagement, too. Days or months ago, he was just your boyfriend; now, you're both wrapping your brains around the exciting, strange, and new concept of "husband and wife." You're beginning to pull away from your family so you can create a new family with your fiancé; it's almost as if you don't quite fit in with your folks the way you used to. You're not one of "the girls" anymore, either. Out at a bar with your single girlfriends, you don't feel as connected with their cosmos-and-cute-guys lives. When a handsome stranger flirts with you, you feel guilty because you're now an engaged woman. "I don't even recognize my own life anymore!" is a thought that crosses the mind of many brides-to-be.

Engaged women can bring order to their inner emotional chaos by becoming aware of the natural psychological process going on within them. (Just knowing that the "unbridely" feelings of sadness and fear have meaning and purpose often helps them release the pressure valve.) In this book, you'll learn how to work through your difficult feelings and grow from them, so that when your wedding day arrives, you'll feel like kicking up your heels to do the electric slide. On your wedding day, you'll be smiling at all your guests—the same way those toothsome brides are smiling out at you from the pages of the bridal magazines today.

Fantasy: *Your engagement will be love and romance, 24/7.*

Reality: This *is* a romantic time of life—choosing a ring, planning your dream wedding, imagining the future stretched out before you. But it's a stressful time for your relationship with your fiancé as well. Many engaged couples report more fighting and less sex, more uncertainty and less fun.

Why? This happens because your relationship has taken on a new seriousness and permanence, and that's just plain scary.

What's more, your relationship, once intensely private, has now become public property. Everyone feels compelled to comment on whether or not you're a good match. Your nosy (and tactless) aunt Betty may shamelessly inquire, "Will he be able to provide for you in the manner to which you are accustomed, dear?" (*That* sure didn't happen when you were dating.) On top of that, all eyes are on you to plan the perfect wedding.

As you and your fiancé have clashing visions of what "perfect" is, you're discovering personality differences and relationship challenges that never came up when you were just dating. You may also be buying cars and homes together, and as you sign both of your names on the dotted line, you're learning about each other on a whole new level, finding out about new strengths and weaknesses, idiosyncrasies and quirks, angels and devils within each other. "What I want is for someone else to plan our wedding for us," Erica commented to me. "And then we'll do it again in five years, when we're settled into marriage and know each other even better."

Engagement is a time of turbulence for many engaged couples, and it doesn't make for 100 percent romance, 100 percent of the time.

Fantasy: *Once engaged, the decision to marry your fiancé is final.*

Reality: Actually, during your engagement, you evaluate your fiancé and the relationship all over again, with even more intensity. "I know in my bones that I want to marry Dan, and I said yes without hesitation," Erica told me. "But I'm finding myself being hypercritical of him and sometimes even second-guessing my decision to marry him."

Why? Think back to when you were just boyfriend and girlfriend, when the possibility always existed that he might bolt when the topic of marriage came up. Self-protectively, you may have held yourself back from fully imagining a lifetime together.

Now that he's about to become your husband, a future with your fiancé has become very real, and you're (understandably) looking at him with a more critical eye. You take note of the good (how caring, loving, expressive, generous, big-hearted, sexy, great with kids, compassionate, [insert your fiancé's fab qualities here]), the bad (his aggressive driving and lead foot, the way he runs when his mommy calls), and the ugly. As Suzanne Finnamore wrote in her novel about a bride-to-be, *Otherwise Engaged*, "Michael leaves his socks on the floor when he takes off his shoes after work. This used to be fine. But now a sock on the floor isn't just a sock on the floor. It's a sock on the floor for the rest of my life."

Brides-to-be often blow these nitpicky moments way out of proportion. They're quick to assume that if they're having these thoughts, it must mean that they have cold feet about getting married. But that's not always true.

Agreeing to marry your fiancé — even as enthusiastically, excitedly, and joyfully as you did — in fact initiates another evaluation process. Yes, chances are you're absolutely going to marry him and you're going to have a great life together, but right now, during your engagement, you're still in a thinking-feeling-exploring process. So it's normal to put your relationship under the microscope all over again. Think of it this way: each time you dissect and analyze your fiancé and your relationship and you *still* want to marry him, you're recommitting yourself to the marriage again.

Fantasy: *You will feel supported and surrounded by your family.*

Reality: "Sometimes, I feel closer to my parents than I have in years as we plan the wedding together," Erica told me during our phone consultation. "At other times, I want to kill them. They're pushing for an over-the-top wedding—a seated, four-course meal served by white-gloved waiters. Dan and I want something without all the pomp and circumstance. The four of us can't come to an agreement, and we're driving each other crazy!"

Like many brides-to-be, Erica was going head-to-head with her parents over the wedding details, but formal vs. casual wasn't the only thing they were fighting about. Beneath the surface was the unspoken, underlying issue they were in conflict over: the change in the family dynamic caused by Erica's impending marriage.

Why? On Erica's wedding day, Dan would become her new legal family; her parents would slip into the number two spot. And they were already feeling the effect; they weren't getting the same amount of attention and affection they'd always gotten from her. Dan was.

When brides-to-be begin to put their future spouses first during the engagement, families often act up and act out. They channel their feelings of abandonment, fear, and sadness about the impending loss of their child into the wedding. When Erica stuck to her guns about not having white-gloved waiters at their wedding, her parents took that as a betrayal, as a rejection of them.

Choosing your fiancé over your family is the healthy, right

thing to do. Like the earlier adolescent rebellion you may have had against your parents, this, too, is another developmental milestone on the road to adulthood and independence. Still, it can be scary and painful for a bride-to-be. Redirecting your attention, affection, and loyalty away from your parents and toward your fiancé hurts your family. And causing your flesh and blood to feel pain makes you feel guilty. So to distance yourself from your guilt, you may pull away from your family by having less contact with them or — the more popular option — by picking fights with them.

It's important to remember that your family's going through a lot, too. They're coming face-to-face with the new reality that soon they'll be losing some of their closeness to you. And, simply put, it hurts to lose any degree of closeness with someone you love, especially a daughter or a sibling. Since most people aren't comfortable openly expressing hurt and sadness, they, too, will pull away, either by disengaging from the relationship (is your mom not very interested in your wedding, perhaps?) or by throwing up smoke screens (is your dad butting heads with you at every opportunity?). As you pull away from them, they pull away from you, and everyone ends up feeling cut off from those to whom they are closest. The end result is the same: most brides-to-be say they feel alienated from or angry at their families for much of their engagements. In the chapter titled "A Family Affair," we'll discuss how reworking your family bonds can result in powerful personal growth for brides-to-be and deeper, more adult relationships with your parents and siblings.

Fantasy: *Engagement party! Bachelorette party! Bridal shower! Being engaged is all about parties!*

Reality: "As soon as we announced our engagement, everybody wanted to see us and celebrate, which was awesome," Erica told me. "But as soon as the parties were over, I became a total recluse. I thought I was going to be a social butterfly my whole engagement, but I've ended up needing a lot of time alone."

Why? Loosening your grip on your identities as a single woman, daughter, and girlfriend can all be destabilizing to your sense of self. Thus, after the initial excitement of announcing the big news, many brides-to-be go into hibernation so they can adjust to the changes they're experiencing and prepare for the changes they're about to experience in marriage.

Letting others see you go through this, warts and all, is often very difficult. "I didn't want to tell my fiancé I was feeling sad," explained Erica. "It didn't seem fair to him that I was feeling this way, since it really had nothing to do with him. And I didn't want to talk to my parents or my close friends about it, either. I didn't want them to get a bad impression of our relationship or think I was having any doubts. So I'm feeling really isolated, which is not how I expected to feel during my engagement." Processing these changes requires space and time to yourself. Be sure to take it.

Tools You'll Need to Be Emotionally Engaged

As you embark upon the process of becoming emotionally engaged, you'll need a few simple things to help you reflect upon and explore your feelings.

A compassionate ear. Talking through your contradictory feelings of joy, excitement, sadness, and fear with a trusted friend or family member will help you gain deeper insight into your emotions. It feels safer, too; exploring difficult emotions is less frightening in the presence of an understanding listener.

Choosing the right person is key. Select someone who is nonjudgmental and patient, a person who can understand that you can be happy *and* sad *and* scared, all at the same time. Your confidante's job is to help you explore your feelings and gain insight into why you might be feeling this way. Their job is *not* to "solve" your problems, "fix" your feelings, or tell you that "you should be happy." (If you hear the latter, move on to another friend and try to accept that some people can't handle the emotional complexity of this "happy" time of your life.)

Your first instinct may be to ask your fiancé to play this role for you. But he may not be the most objective sounding board in this situation. Your roller coaster–like emotions may unnerve and upset him, causing him to react (or worse, overreact) to your normal and natural—yet unsettling—feelings. You don't want to keep secrets from him, but you may want to put off sharing your deepest, darkest, rawest thoughts until after you've processed them. Saying something like, "Just in case you've been feeling my distance recently, I want to share what I've been going through. Don't worry: it has nothing to do with you or us or the wedding. I've just been feeling sad about growing up and leaving my family.

Can I tell you more about it?" keeps the lines of communication open without threatening the relationship.

If you can't find a compassionate ear, seek out a therapist or mental-health worker; listening—without judging or fixing—is what they're trained to do. It will be money well spent.

A journal. Writing is a powerful tool for self-discovery. When you're overwrought with emotion, the physical act of writing in a journal often offers brides-to-be immediate emotional relief. As you write, the emotions flow out of your body and onto the page, where you can be more objective about them.

Journaling can also give you emotional clarity and deeper understanding. As you write, reflect on what you're writing. Follow the inner dialogue you're having with yourself, and the conversations you're having in your head with others. Become aware of the private fantasies you have. Flesh out ideas. Speculate. Analyze. Explore.

Keep your journal accessible, in your purse or on your bedside table (make sure, however, that your journal is safe, private, and 100 percent confidential). And be sure to have it with you as you work your way through the Emotional To-Do List exercises in this book.

Fantasy: *A wedding is just a big party.*

Reality: How many parties have you attended from which you've gone home with a new husband who has the power to make life-and-death decisions for you, a new branch on your family tree, and (possibly) a new last name?

Why? Enough said.

Fantasy: *Wedding planning shouldn't take over your life.*

Reality: Allowing your wedding planning to take over your life can actually be beneficial in helping you make the transition from single to married. "Before I got engaged, I'd laugh at and ridicule my friends who were obsessed with their weddings," Erica said. "But now I get it. I think about and talk about my wedding all the time. I can't help it!"

Why? Being engrossed with your wedding can be psychologically and emotionally healthy, if you can find the metaphors in all the detailed work you're doing. For example, trying on dress after dress helps you become comfortable in your new skin as a bride. Tweaking your online registry — ten place settings? twelve? ten? twelve? — helps you imagine your new married home (and china closet). Finding the perfect place cards helps you wrap your brain around the fact that all your friends and family will be gathered in one place to celebrate your marriage. All the work you put into your wedding — the countless hours, the flipping through magazines, the dreaming, the scheming, the tasting, the trying on, the making lists, the making calls — helps you process and integrate the identity changes that will occur on your wedding day. Every wedding detail, when you think of it metaphorically, can facilitate your transition from single to married.

So go ahead: be obsessed about your wedding if you want to be. Just bring a psychological awareness to your obsession. Find the metaphor in the puff pastries.

Fantasy: *You can avoid wedding stress and emotional crises by having a brief engagement or by eloping.*

Reality: Nope.

Why? Making the psychological transition from single to married is a process *all* brides-to-be go through. For those with short engagements, the road can be even rockier. They have to take the bumps at high speed, and their emotions tend to run higher, hotter, and faster than those with yearlong engagements. Brief brides-to-be often need more emotional support; in fact, a third of all brides I counsel have engagements that are less than four months long. What about brides who jet off to the Little White Wedding Chapel in Vegas? They have the distinct pleasure of going through the emotional upheaval with a wedding band already on their finger.

Fantasy: *Not every bride-to-be has an identity crisis during her engagement.*

Reality: True, some have them *after* they're married.

Why? Occasionally, I meet married women who don't see the need for bridal counseling. "I don't remember going through anything like that," they say to me. "My engagement was really fun!"

"Well, then, let me ask you," I say, gingerly. "How was your first year of marriage?"

"Oh God, it was rough," they say, shaking their heads. "I ended up spending a lot of nights sleeping alone in the guest room."

I've had this conversation so many times; it tells me that nobody magically jumps from "me" to "we." The psychological transition from single to married—and the identity crisis that accompanies it—must occur at some point, either before the wedding or after.

My advice? Be grateful you're going through this natural and necessary process now, before the wedding. You're avoiding some very lonely nights in the guest room.

The Emotional To-Do List Item #1
Your Fantasies About Being Engaged

 Since you were a little girl, you've likely had clear ideas about what your engagement would be like. These fantasies may be outdated and unrealistic— when you were ten years old, for example, you may have thought that you'd be going out for tea and petit fours all the time with your bridesmaids during your engagement—but today they're affecting your happiness as a bride-to-be at an unconscious level.

If you're unaware that your fantasies sometimes influence your feelings, you may feel sad, guilty, hurt, or disappointed, but not know why. For example, when your fiancé comes home from work without flowers for you—*again*—you may lash out at him. You may be angry because he's not fulfilling your high-school fantasy that life as an engaged woman life would be a steady stream of love poems and long-stemmed roses once you'd found "the one."

Exercise: What fantasies about being engaged are dancing around in your mind? Reflect on the ideas you've had about being a bride-to-be during different eras in your life. Can you remember your first thoughts from when you were a little girl? From junior high, high school, and college? From your first serious relationships? And, more recently, from when you started dating your fiancé, and from the days immediately before and after your fiancé popped the question? Describe your fantasies in your journal.

Articulating your fantasies about your engagement can release you from their grip. Once you're aware of them, you'll be able to notice when you are overreacting because you're comparing your real engagement unfavorably to your fantasy engagement.

Then, describe the reality of your engagement in your journal. In what ways is your engagement matching your fantasies? Failing to live up to your fantasies? Surpassing your fantasies?

Fantasy: *Having cold feet means you must call off your wedding.*

Reality: Not necessarily.

Why? "Cold feet" is a catchall term for the normal fears about getting married that many brides and grooms experience. The key is determining which fears can be worked through and which fears are signs you should call off the wedding.

You can make this distinction by breaking down your cold feet into three categories:

1. *Wedding stress.* How much are your feelings of cold feet due to the pressure to create a picture-perfect wedding? If most of your angst is about the wedding, take steps to control your anxiety. Delegate tasks to trusted friends and family. Scale down your grand vision into

something more meaningful and manageable. Spend the extra bucks on a wedding planner. And remember that the wedding day—and the stress that accompanies it—will soon pass.

2. *Your feelings about getting married—period.* How much are your feelings of cold feet due to your fear of growing up (no matter how old you are)? Of making the final cut of the apron strings and leaving your family? Of ending your single life and losing your identity? Of the unknown that is marriage? If this describes you, read on: in this book, you'll learn how to work through, resolve, and grow from these issues so you can walk down the aisle with a clear and happy conscience.

3. *Your feelings about marrying him—specifically.* How much are your feelings of cold feet due to concerns about your fiancé? His emotional distance or volatility? His work ethic, be it too lax or too strong? His nice but dull-ness? His lavish spending or chronic thriftiness? His drinking or drug use? These are serious concerns, and it's essential to assess, acknowledge, and accept the man you're about to marry for who he really is. If he's the source of your cold feet, you need to bring a cool analytical eye to the relationship so you can determine if a lifetime with him is what's best for you.

Want to evaluate your feelings of cold feet even further? You'll find "Cold Feet Alerts" at the end of this chapter, as well as in chapters 3, 4, 5, and 6.

Going Easy on Yourself

Erica was about to hang up the phone at the end of our conversation when she went on a little rant. "What you're talking about makes complete sense," she said to me. "So why didn't I think of this before? Why did I put on a happy face when what I really felt was sad and scared and anxious?"

"Whoa, whoa," I said to her. "Slow down."

Brides-to-be, I've discovered, are masters at beating themselves up. They first beat themselves up for not being happy enough during their engagements. Then, they beat themselves up for not knowing it's okay to not be 100 percent happy. It's a no-win situation.

"Be gentle with yourself," I said to Erica. "Go easy. Don't judge yourself. You've got a lot on your plate right now — don't add more stress to your life!"

"I'm creating a problem here, aren't I?" she said.

Indeed, she was. As a busy bride-to-be, Erica needed to pick her battles, and battling with herself was something she didn't need to do. She needed to focus on the emotional tasks at hand, which included facing the end of her single life and changes in her relationships with her family, friends, and fiancé. Erica needed to go easy on herself, and you do too.

Cold Feet Alert: Signs You Should Call It Off

 Over the years, I've consulted with many brides- and grooms-to-be as they decided whether to call off a wedding, and I've discovered this tragic fact: too many people talk themselves into getting married even when they know it's wrong because (a) they're afraid of being the bad guy, and (b) they're afraid of causing their fiancé(e) pain. These are two terrible reasons to say "I do."

If any of the following twenty quotes I've heard from brides (and grooms) have crossed your mind, it may be time to return the ring and cancel the caterer—before you make a painful, damaging, and expensive mistake that can only be ameliorated by divorce:

1. "Calling it off would be embarrassing for me, him, and our families. I can't do it to all of us."
2. "I feel like my fiancé makes my life more difficult and drains me instead of making my life easier and filling me up."
3. "When I had a dress fitting, for the first time in my life I broke out in hives, just like that scene in *Sex and the City*."
4. "We've gone too far with the wedding planning to call it off now."
5. "My parents have spent too much money. They'll kill me."
6. "I can see myself having an affair two, five, ten years down the road."
7. "There's a little voice inside me that says, 'Don't go through with it.'"
8. "I'm looking for an excuse to call the wedding off."
9. "I'm being a major bitch to him. I'm trying to drive him to call it off because I don't want to be the bad guy."
10. "I gave him an ultimatum, and a part of me will always be worried that we're getting married because I threatened to break up with him if we didn't."

11. "He feels more like a friend than a lover and partner. We're comfortable together, but we don't have the passion I've always wanted to have in my marriage. He's Mr. Good Enough, not necessarily Mr. Right."

12. "We haven't had sex in two years."

13. "I'm afraid of his anger."

14. "I don't respect his work ethic. I've paid off my graduate-school loans and work really hard; he's dillydallying through his PhD and ringing up massive debt."

15. "I don't feel old enough to get married."

16. "I haven't been on my own long enough to get married."

17. "I don't feel ready to settle down the way he wants to—buy a house, have kids, the whole thing. I want to focus on my career."

18. "We got engaged too fast. I wasn't ready, but I said yes anyway."

19. "I feel like I owe it to him to get married."

20. "My fiancé's such a great person; I don't want to cause him pain."

The Emotional To-Do List Item #2
Considering Calling Off Your Wedding?

Here are three ways to help you clarify your decision:

1. *Imagine calling it off.* I ask every cold-footed bride- or groom-to-be to fantasize about calling off their wedding. For some, "going there" instantly helps them realize that they don't want to cancel the nuptials or end the relationship. Others have the opposite reaction. One bride-

to-be recently told me, "Oh my God, I feel huge relief when I think about calling it off." Her body relaxed; she was able to breathe and feel grounded again. Now it's your turn: imagine calling off your own wedding. (Telling your fiancé will be difficult, but for this exercise, assume that you've already done it.) Inhale and exhale deeply, letting this idea sink in. How do you feel? What are the exact words that cross your mind? Be honest with yourself. Listen to that "little voice" inside you—your inner wisdom, your intuition.

2. *Put yourself in your fiancé's shoes.* Ask yourself this simple question: Would you want to marry someone who had to talk themselves into marrying you? When I asked one cold-footed groom-to-be this question, he said, "Oh, no. She deserves much, much better than that."

3. *Determine "should" vs. "want."* Is getting married to this person what you *should* do? (Have you heard yourself say, "I owe it to him," or "I don't want to embarrass him," or "I'm afraid to cause him pain?") Or is marrying him what you *want* to do? You've gotta want this marriage; now is not the time for "shoulds."

Stage One

ENDING

CHAPTER 3

The Last First Kiss
Grieving the End of Your Single Life

"The night after we got engaged, after the whirlwind of calling friends and telling people our great news, Dave and I wanted a quiet Friday together," Rachel, who you may remember from chapter 1, told a workshop of brides-to-be. "We went to the grocery store, rented a movie, and were looking forward to a night of hanging out, just the two of us.

"We were in the dairy aisle when I saw her," she remembered. Rachel recognized a woman from her gym, a professional-looking woman just like herself, carrying a Coach purse and pushing a shopping cart. She was wearing her gym clothes and picking out yogurt from the dairy case.

"She sent me into a panic attack," said Rachel, "because just a few months earlier, that was *me*."

Before Rachel met Dave, she had settled into a Friday-night routine to wind down from a grueling week of work as a systems analyst at a bank. She'd work out at the gym, stock up at the grocery, make a dinner of yogurt and cereal, and plop in front of the TV to watch *Trading Spaces*. She'd completely relax and let down her guard as she puttered around by herself in her pj's, wearing a cleansing mask on her face and painting her toenails. She loved her Friday nights alone at home, even if, from time to time, they could be a little lonely.

Engaged for only twenty-four hours, with her beautiful husband-to-be by her side and a sparkling diamond ring on her finger, Rachel had what she'd always dreamed of. "But I looked at that woman, and I was *jealous* of her," Rachel recalled. "She looked so independent, content just taking care of herself, going about her business. And here I was, finally engaged to a wonderful man, and all I wanted was my old life back." Trailing behind Dave through the aisles, Rachel's spirits nose-dived.

Rachel didn't want to feel sad on her second day as an engaged woman, so she banished the negative feelings. She compartmentalized them. In her imagination, she locked her sadness up into a little box and threw away the key. The result? In the weeks that followed, Rachel felt very little. Neither overjoyed nor overwhelmed, Rachel felt flat, which was no way, she thought, for a bride-to-be to feel.

The Sudden Impact of Engagement

From the moment you got engaged, you, like Rachel, have likely been confronted on a daily, even hourly, basis with how your life has already changed. You run into a guy friend who asks you, "Hey, Jonesie! Can I still call you 'Jonesie' after you get married?" Out at a bar with your single girlfriends, you don't feel as connected with their daily dating dramas. When you get good news at work, you instinctively call your mom, but midconversation you realize that you should have called your fiancé first. It's in these small realizations that you notice how your life, your identity, and your relationships are already changing now that you're engaged.

Officially, you're a "fiancée," but your primary identity today is still a single woman — that's who you are, and what you feel like. You will eventually evolve into a married woman, but before you can begin to do that, you must first loosen your ties to your identity of single woman. For many brides-to-be, letting go of this identity can feel as powerful as grief, like a death of their single selves, and grieving during the "happiest" time of your life can be grueling.

When you're grieving, it's normal to feel a whole host of emotions, all at full blast. Why? Because your defenses, which normally keep strong emotions at bay, are weakened, allowing torrents of feelings to flood in; the lid is torn off the container, so to speak. Sadness, introspection, and weepiness rush in. Anger, frustration, anxiety, and fear flood your system. Confusion, disorientation, and disappointment are common. Add to the mix the pressure every bride feels to be happy, and it's no surprise that sane women become bitchy bridezillas. The emotional overload — on top of planning a wedding — can sometimes be simply too much for one bride-to-be to handle.

Some try to avoid this by willing themselves to feel *only* happy. After all, to paraphrase Cyndi Lauper, brides-to-be just wanna have fun. Unfortunately, emotions don't work that way. When you pick and choose what emotions you're willing to let in—when you say yes to happiness and no to everything else—you end up shutting off what I call "the feeling system."

To understand feelings as a system is to understand that your emotions are interconnected and interdependent. And, as in any system—a car, say, or a computer—if one component doesn't work properly, the whole system works less efficiently, or not at all.

Rachel shut her feeling system off the moment she put her fear and anxiety into that imaginary box. She couldn't feel happy because she refused to let in her fear. Turning the feeling system off like that causes you to feel neither high nor low, but instead an emotional flatness, an absence of any feeling. You certainly don't feel authentically happy, and that's the major concern expressed by most engaged women.

Rachel desperately wanted to feel the happiness she knew was in her heart about marrying Dave. But authentic happiness is spontaneous and alive, and spontaneity requires an openness to whatever emotions arise. To feel genuinely happy, Rachel had to risk feeling her "negative" emotions. She had to be willing to feel her fear, as well as any sadness or anger that lurked there. She had to turn her feeling system on again. That's what it means to be "emotionally engaged": feeling all your emotions as they arise—the grip of fear, the pit-in-your-stomach sorrow, the spikes of anger—enables you to also feel authentic happiness about being engaged.

Grieving for your single life goes on for much of your engagement, but that doesn't mean it's doom and gloom 24/7. In fact, it's just the opposite: by letting your sadness and fear work through you, you'll actually feel more fully alive. And happier, too. This chapter will explore different ways brides-to-be experience the end of their single lives, and you'll get the tools you need to help you move through this normal, natural, and necessary grieving process that prepares you for married life.

Saying Good-bye to the Girl About Town

A seaplane dropped Cynthia and Brian in a cove of Kodiak Island. The plan: four romantic, isolated, fun-filled summertime days of sea kayaking and camping in the pristine Alaskan wilderness.

Paddling along the shoreline, they passed grizzly bears and cubs feasting on wild salmon. Yet despite the beautiful scenery, after a while Cynthia's arms began to ache from paddling, and the sight of the hungry bears became more than a little unsettling to her.

The second night of their trip, there was a driving rainstorm. Soggy and cold, with a headlamp strapped across her forehead, Cynthia rolled out their sleeping bags in the tent. She was feeling miserable and more than a little sorry for herself. "This vacation is hard," she muttered under her breath.

As Brian zipped the tent closed for the night, Cynthia froze. A bear was rustling around their camp, she thought. Terrified, she stared at Brian, trying to transmit through her worried look a silent warning signal about the bear.

But Brian interpreted her look differently. "Will you marry me?" he asked, a shy smile of anticipation on his face.

This major moment of her life was truly a moment of terror. Not only had Brian asked the question that both attracted and repelled her, but also a killer grizzly might be just one flimsy zipper away from them.

"Yes," Cynthia replied frantically, "but will you first go listen for that bear?"

She didn't sleep a wink that night. To this day, she still isn't sure if it was her fear of a bear attack or her fear about getting married that kept her wide awake.

Before the Alaskan adventure, Cynthia and Brian's relationship had been a nine-month whirlwind. The couple quickly discovered not only a deep physical attraction and passion between them, but shared values, dreams, and goals in life. They were perfect together. And after years of bachelorhood, Brian was ready, willing, and able to get married. Cynthia was too. She had mixed and mingled at happy hours and black-tie fund-raisers on the Chicago singles' scene for the past twelve years. She had organized groups of friends for ski trips and summer time-shares. She'd had the occasional hookup and a few serious, verging-on-marriage relationships. She'd "done" the single life, and she'd had enough.

Or so she thought. Her frightened reaction to Brian's proposal unnerved her: Did it mean he wasn't Mr. Right, after all? Or was her response a "normal" one?

As she paddled her sea kayak the next day, Cynthia couldn't make heads or tails of her emotions because her fear of getting married would come and go. One moment she was overjoyed, finding herself grinning from ear to ear and feeling as if she might burst with joy. The next, she felt sick to her stomach with anxiety, sick over the idea of planning their wedding. Her feelings swung back and forth between elated and terrified for the rest of the trip.

Returning home helped her settle into her new reality as an engaged woman. Their families and friends were delighted by the news, and their enthusiasm was infectious. As Cynthia became caught up in the celebratory mood, her fears dissipated.

Then, one Saturday night, as Cynthia was getting dressed to go out to a formal dinner party hosted by some of Brian's married friends, she found she was in a funky, bad mood. She was irritated but didn't know why. She had been looking forward to the party all week, glad for another opportunity to get to know Brian's circle of friends better. "There's no reason for me to be unhappy tonight," she thought to herself.

Her mind wandered to her gang of single friends, who had gone skiing in Vail for the weekend. "They're getting off the slopes just about now," she thought. "Going out for beers and that ridiculous après-ski dancing in ski parkas and pants. And I'm stuck going to a stuffy adult dinner party." In that moment, it felt to Cynthia that she was joining what the über-single-girl character Bridget Jones called the "smug marrieds." In nine months flat, Cynthia had gone from girl about town to smug married-to-be. When she thought about it that way, she felt whiplashed.

And sad, too. As she looked into the mirror to apply her makeup, Cynthia knew that deep down she was happy about marrying Brian, but at that moment she was sad, sad, sad.

Her life as a single woman was over. Forever. No more wondering who she'd meet around the next corner. No more going out to the deli to pick up lunch and returning to the office with a date for drinks. No more first dates. No more first kisses. No more anticipatory anxiety about whether a new guy would call, and no more jolts of excitement when his name popped up on her caller ID. Her girl-about-town life was over.

Her life as a single woman wasn't solely about the booms and busts of dating, of course. It was about Cynthia living life on her own, independently, accountable to no one. Since graduating from college, Cynthia had created a good life for herself. Her career in sales was fast-paced, satisfying, and lucrative. She'd developed a strong network of friends and a vast community of acquaintances. She'd learned how to face life on her own and how to depend on herself. Through it all, she'd become a confident, strong, happy person.

Cynthia watched herself in the mirror as a big tear rolled down her cheek. Then she started to sob, consumed by a sadness she had never expected to feel when she used to picture herself engaged to Brian. The pit in her stomach grew as she thought about her friends skiing in Colorado without her; about all the single-girl adventures and debacles she wouldn't have ever again; about all that she had learned, discovered, and done as a woman on her own; about the fact that her life as she'd always known it was over.

She didn't want Brian to see her tears, so she pulled herself together and applied her mascara. "Smug marrieds, here I come," she thought to herself.

The dinner party turned out to be fun. Sitting beside Brian reassured Cynthia that marrying him was what she wanted. Every time they exchanged knowing glances or shared a private joke—even when she brushed his knee under the table—she was reassured that they were on the right track. (And the smug marrieds were hardly smug. Despite their fancy wedding crystal and china, the evening was plenty wild with drinking and dancing, an atmosphere that helped Cynthia feel right at home.) Still, she couldn't square the two contradictory ideas that she was both happy about getting married to Brian and sad about the end of her single life. Later that week, she found my Web site and called me for a phone session.

When I explained that it was healthy for her to grieve the ending of her single life and that it was in fact preparing her to take on her new identity as a married woman, Cynthia did what all brides-to-be who call me do: she breathed a big sigh of relief. "You mean you've heard this before?" she asked.

"All the time," I replied. "And I went through it myself, big time."

Cynthia was experiencing grief, plain and simple. Unexpressed grief can begin as a feeling of indefinite, irksome annoyance. You feel perturbed and short-tempered. You're in a foul mood for no apparent reason. Most brides-to-be try to push the discomfort down or ignore it, hoping that it will magically go away. But grief over the ending of a formative period of your life can't be wished or willed away. It must be experienced before it can be integrated. You have to feel it before you can move beyond it.

It helps to think of powerful emotions like waves in the ocean. Say, for instance, that you feel a twinge of sadness. Since you only want to feel happy, you do your damnedest to ignore it. Over time, however, the sadness builds in critical mass, the same way a wave grows in size as it approaches the shore. Emotionally, you start feeling more anxious, irritable, and short-tempered.

What you need to do is let the wave of sadness crash over you, and you need to feel it. Having a good cry releases all that tension. The sadness subsides. It dissipates in power the same way a wave loses strength as it rolls onto the shore. As you connect to the sadness, you'll feel more calm and at peace. You'll be able to reflect on the emotional experience and learn from its meaning and purpose.

That's what happened to Cynthia before the dinner party. Her funky, bad mood was a cover for a deeper sadness that had been building, growing in mass and strength, so to speak, since Brian first proposed to her that rainy night in the tent. Once Cynthia let her tears fall—once she connected to the feeling—she was able to make an important intuitive leap: she was crying about the end of her single days. This is the meaning-making component of emotional work; it's how you learn from your emotions so that you're not just at their whim. By finally letting her sadness in, it moved through her. It was over, and Cynthia was able to be fully present for the fun at the dinner party.

"I'm glad that's over with," Cynthia said to me. "So what happens now?"

Understandably, all brides-to-be are in a hurry when it comes to working through their difficult emotions. Grieving the end of your single life isn't a one-shot deal, however. You may have sporadic moments of grief throughout your engagement. Your grief may rise up and kick you in the butt when you least expect it. When you sleep by yourself in your own bed instead of at his place, you may become overwhelmed by the thought of moving out. When you're on a tight deadline at the office and your fiancé is whining for your time and attention, you may miss the days when you only had to worry about yourself and your career. Or when you're heading to a dinner party while your single pals are going barhopping, you may find yourself being mad at your fiancé for taking you away from the life you knew. Grief's like that; you never know what might trigger it.

Allowing the sadness in as it occurs will help you process the ending of your single life. It will help you let go of your single identity and make room for your new identity as a married woman. Doing grief work during your engagement is essential.

Before we hung up the phone, Cynthia made another important connection. "Maybe my freak-out about bears when Brian proposed was more about my fear of this ending," she said to me. "Maybe on some level, I knew I was afraid to give up the single life I've always known. Maybe I was making the bears up. Maybe there weren't any outside the tent at all."

The Emotional To-Do List Item #3
Reflecting on Your Single Life

 What aspects of your single life are you sad to see ending? What parts of your identity as a single woman are you scared to give up? What aspects of your single life are you relieved and happy to see coming to a close?

In your journal, write in detail about your feelings regarding this ending, or talk through it with a friend. The power of your sadness, fear, joy, and relief may surprise you, so be open to anything that arises.

If I Knew *Then* What I Know *Now* . . .
Is All This Emotional Stuff Really *Necessary?*

During my engagement, I couldn't seem to pay attention to myself and my feelings. When we went to city hall to get our marriage license, for example, I decided to take Jon's last name on the spur of the moment. I had tried to think it through beforehand, but it got me too worked up. So I made a last-minute decision that I still regret. I've been married almost a year, and the name change has been eating away at me for months.

—Suzanne, married ten months

I loved planning our wedding, and I let it take up ninety percent of my free time. I was totally into being creative, designing the invitations, color-coordinating the whole day, learning calligraphy. But I know now that I should have been taking my marriage as seriously as I took my conversations with the florist.

On our wedding day, I played the role of the bride, and I was happy because I was living out the fantasy I had created. But I was emotionally disconnected from my husband. I remember thinking during our first dance, "Can people see that I'm not as happy as I should be? I hope I can fool them." It was awful.

If I could do it again, I'd forget most of the fluffy stuff I was focused on and put my energy into the emotional aspects of the wedding, the marriage, and myself.

—*Nellie, married one year*

The End of Just Me and My Career

"One month before Jake proposed, I felt totally confident about getting married to him," Sarah, a thirty-five-year-old sociology professor, told me during a phone consultation. "The day after he proposed, I felt mortal terror. Whenever I told somebody the news, I could barely get the words out."

Sarah had been engaged for two months, and she'd developed what she called "an obsession" with her diamond engagement ring. On some days, the stone was too big. On others, it was too small. Occasionally, it was just right, but that feeling of contentment was rare and fleeting.

Sarah repeatedly told me how beautiful the ring was. She and her fiancé had designed it themselves. They drew sketches on the back of napkins one night at a bar soon after they got engaged. Later, they found the perfect stone. Jake took great pride in the ring—how big the stone was and the fact that they had created the ring together—and it brought him immense pleasure to see it on her hand. But Sarah couldn't get used to the sight of it on her. "It's disorienting to look down at my hands," she said. "They're not my hands; they're the hands of a married woman."

Her ring made her uncomfortable, especially around her colleagues in the sociology department. "Yesterday I was at an academic conference, and I tucked my hand under my arm to hide my ring," she told me. "I felt really exposed with my big diamond ring on."

Angsting about her ring made Sarah annoyed with herself because she knew in her heart and soul that she wanted to marry Jake. Every time she searched for red flags about him or the relationship, she came up empty-handed. The night before calling me, she had even gone so far as to create a pro/con list. "I ended up with ten totally positive pros for why we should get married and four piddling little cons," she said.

The detail in Sarah's story that really jumped out at me was that she felt most ambivalent about the ring in the presence of her colleagues at the university.

"I hadn't noticed that," she said. "But you're right. I feel most self-conscious about my ring when I'm at work."

"Why do you think that is?" I asked.

"Well, when my colleague saw it, he said, 'Wow, big ring. It's bigger than what I gave my wife,'" she recounted. "Another colleague looked directly at it and didn't say a thing. That made me feel even more insecure. Did she also think it was too big? Too much? Does she think we're rich? Is she envious? Is she judging me? Is she taking me less seriously as a scholar?"

"What does it mean to you to be a sociologist with a big diamond engagement ring?" I asked.

"It means I'm no longer like them," she told me. "I'm no longer *just* a sociologist, which is how I've thought of myself for the last twelve years."

Sarah readily admitted that her identity, self-image, and self-worth were entirely wrapped up in her work as an academic. She'd kept her nose in the books throughout her undergraduate years, master's, and PhD, with her eye always on her goal of a tenure-track teaching position. She'd attained her post through sheer hard work. She was proud of her achievements.

Marriage required an adjustment, an expansion of her self-image. She would have to add "wife" and "married woman" to her identity. Perhaps her diamond ring was a symbol of these changes.

"When I wear the ring around my colleagues, it's proof that (a) I'm marrying 'outside of the tribe,' because most academics have modest wedding bands and this is a bigger, showier ring, and (b) not only will I soon become a wife, but likely a mother, too. We are planning on having kids right away. So maybe wearing the ring at work brings me face-to-face with how much in my life is changing. I feel like I'm being torn away from the academic world. After working so hard to get into it and feeling so proud about what I've done as a sociologist, it feels really painful to let that identity go."

"It's not so much about letting the identity of sociologist

go," I told her, "but expanding your identity to include that of wife and then mother."

"But what'll happen to 'sociologist me'?" Sarah snapped back. "Who am I if I'm not just 'Sarah the Sociologist'?"

For the first time since she got engaged, Sarah was tapping into her fear, sadness, and even anger about the changes her marriage to Jake would inevitably bring about. Her focus on the ring had been a clever distraction from the changes she was facing.

Sarah had hit a core issue that many brides-to-be struggle with. Who are you now as you let go of your identity as a single woman to make room for your new identity as a married woman? In this in-between time of being engaged, neither single nor married, many brides-to-be feel a rupture with their former realities. This can be disturbing to your sense of self since it requires you to let your old way of life die; only by giving up your single life do you create the opportunity to enter married life. Who you are as a person doesn't fundamentally change—you're still you, of course—but you have to form a new relationship to yourself as a married woman. The part of you that clings to your solo, single identity and complete independence must fade so that you can become an interdependent married person. Engagement is a time of disintegration of the old identity so that reintegration of the new identity as a married woman can eventually occur.

These ideas resonated with Sarah, she said, because they were reflected in a dream that she recently had. "In my dream, I had lost my driver's license," she said. "I was frantically searching all my pockets and tearing up my town house looking for it. I woke up feeling really scared, and I couldn't shake the feeling all day."

I asked her what she thought the dream meant.

"Well, I need my driver's license to drive, obviously, and to prove who I am when I get on an airplane or buy alcohol," she told me. "*Oh* . . . it's proof of identification. Of my identity."

For Sarah, the symbolism of this dream couldn't be more clear: on a deep level, she felt like she had lost her identity. The dream confirmed what she had discovered earlier in our conversation: loosening her ties to her old identity of Sarah the Sociologist so that she could later form a new relationship with herself as a sociologist, wife, and mother was causing her to feel unmoored and lost. "It's the end of my career-minded way of life as I know it," she said. "And while I know it's what I want, it's still a lot to absorb."

Sarah's insights helped her take the focus off her diamond engagement ring and put it back onto herself and the identity change that she, as a bride-to-be, was going through. She hung up the phone at the end of our session feeling relieved. Not only was what she was going through normal, but she was on the right track.

One month later, Sarah called me up for another session. "I've been up and down," she said. "I'm forcing myself to focus less on the ring and more on myself. Sometimes I get really sad about ending my solo-minded life, my single focus on my career. But at other times, I'm really happy. Last night, Jake and I started moving his ugly 'guy' furniture—heavy wooden tables, a huge La-Z-Boy—into my feminine little house, and it was really fun. We laughed a ton and it made us both happy.

"I also realize that getting married to Jake is giving me the confidence to look beyond academia and explore other ways to use my degree," she continued. "I'm thinking about work in ways I never would have entertained without him. So I'm finally seeing how being married to Jake opens me up to new identities—a new career direction, possibly, along with 'wife' and 'mother.' After a month of feeling sad about the end of being just Sarah the Sociologist, I'm coming to see the positive value of getting married—*finally!*"

Another dream that Sarah had had a few days earlier confirmed this to her. In the dream she was inside a grand, empty house by herself. Wind was howling outside, and she had battened down the hatches to ride out the storm. A woman wearing a housedress was knocking on the front door. She wanted to be let inside the house to escape the storm. In the dream, Sarah was terrified to let her in, but she did so anyway. When the woman entered, Sarah felt at peace. The terror she'd expected to feel in the presence of this woman didn't materialize. In fact, being in the same room as the woman in the housedress calmed Sarah down.

What did she make of the dream? I asked.

"There were a lot of similarities between me and the woman," she said. "She had my same dark, curly hair. But she was wearing a housedress, which only housewives wear, so I think she symbolizes the emerging 'wife' part of me.

"I think the dream was speaking to my fear of the wife

role," she continued. "It's telling me that when I let it in—when I let 'wife' become a part of my identity in addition to 'sociologist'—I'll feel at peace."

With her wedding two months away, Sarah took comfort in this dream. Although she hadn't yet embraced her new identity of wife, she had let that identity into her house, so to speak—into herself. Sarah felt she was on the way to wifehood, and she felt good and happy about that.

The Emotional To-Do List Item #4
Tracking Your Dreams

 Your dream life offers access to your unconscious, or to hidden parts of yourself—feelings, opinions, ways of being, emotional movement, and growth that you're not yet aware of. Dreams tap into your deepest inner emotional and psychological workings and offer you greater insight into yourself.

Once you get the hang of it, working with your dreams can become a creative and invaluable aspect of your emotional work.

Before you fall asleep at night, open your journal to an empty page and keep a pen at the ready. If you are awakened by a dream, roll over and write down key words and images from the dream. This will help you recall it in the morning.

When you wake up, try to awaken slowly so as not to lose the delicate threads that give you access to your nightly dreams. Lie still and play your dream over in your mind like a movie. Then write down everything you can remember about your dream before you get out of bed—the who, what, where, why, and how of your dream.

Throughout your day, let the dream images play over in your mind. Observe what thoughts, insights, and connections you make to the dream. Keep in mind that your dream images are all clues to what's really going on inside you. For example, if you dream of your mom, the dream is likely either commenting on your feelings about your mother or helping you to access the mothering part of your personality.

Who are the figures in your dream? What is the setting of your dream? What is the predominant mood of the dream? How did you feel when you woke up? What images interest and intrigue you the most? What thoughts, ideas, feelings, and associations do you make to those images?

What could this dream be telling you about yourself that you don't already know? Keep track of your dreams as you go through your engagement and observe how they reflect the changes you're going through.

Packing It In

Moving had never been a major trauma for Pauline. In fact, she was that rare bird who actually enjoyed the process of searching for the perfect apartment, packing up her belongings, and starting anew. It had always been more of an adventure than a source of stress for Pauline.

That is, until she packed to move into her fiancé's apartment just before their wedding. This move was unlike all the others. "I had a very keen awareness that I would be unpacking my boxes as a married person, and that alone was enough to send me off the deep end," said Pauline.

For Pauline, the line between single life and married life

was very distinct. She'd never lived with a guy before, so she was crossing over that line into marriage. "No longer would I be single," she remembers thinking as she packed. "My life would be entwined with somebody else's. I could no longer make decisions that affected only me. I was anticipating having somebody around all the time. It was a lot to get used to."

Pauline's feelings about ending her single life became crystal clear as she sorted through her belongings. Throughout the move, she had two empty boxes. One box was marked TO MOVE, the other SALVATION ARMY. To make it into the TO MOVE box, every item had to earn its way; otherwise it was donated.

"I stood in the middle of the living room and sobbed over a three-foot-tall teddy bear that someone had given me years ago, which didn't really fit into a guy's apartment," Pauline recalled. "I was surprised at how strong my feelings were. It felt kind of crazy at first, but then I realized I wasn't just moving; I was sorting through my entire life.

"And I felt like I was boxing up a portion of my life that I could never return to. Giving certain objects away—an insignificant little trinkety teacuppy thing that someone had given me when I was in junior high that clearly wasn't going to make the cut—made me feel like I was 'giving away' part of my childhood.

"Even though I was looking forward to getting married, during that move I felt like I was saying good-bye to a huge part of my life," she continued. "I was very, very sad to say good-bye."

The physical act of packing boxes helped Pauline connect

with, express, process, and work through her feelings. "The practical side of packing up my life was really a way to close the door on singleness—to 'finish' the season of singleness for me—and to prepare to reopen the door to married life," she remembered. "I also realized that I didn't have to give away everything. My most treasured memories and things would come with me. I was bringing who I was—and who I'd been—to my new home with Drew and my marriage.

"Taping up the boxes gave me a tangible end, and opening them up at Drew's gave me a tangible, clean, new start," she concluded. "I think the simple process of opening boxes with Drew and then blending our things together offered me a new look at how I fit into his life. Before I moved in, I had trouble picturing how my stuff would mesh with his, how I would even find room for my stuff in his place. Unpacking was a lesson in how our lives would blend together. Unpacking was a joy that made me excited about discovering who the 'me' was that I brought over the marriage threshold."

The Emotional To-Do List Item #5
A Ritual to Honor Your Single Life

 You may want to mark this major transition out of your single world by honoring it with a private ritual. A ritual can be elaborate or simple, but the effect is the same: to bring an unusually focused attention, concentration, and mindfulness to what you are doing, which can lead to a greater sense of closure.

For this ritual, gather together items that symbolize your single life—your apartment or car keys, for example. Your business card. Your little black book. Items associated with old boyfriends—gifts, photos, love letters, CDs. Your Match.com account information. Include all items that are symbolic of this time in your life that has been about just you.

Create a tranquil, contemplative atmosphere for this ritual. Consider creating an altar of sorts to place your single-life items on; you may want to set them on a beautiful piece of fabric or surround them with candles. Place a vase of flowers beside you. Play music that reminds you of your single life, of your past, of what you've been through. Dim the lights. Make this time special, even sacred.

Sit before your altar of single-life items and reflect on each, one at a time. Hold each one and reflect on the "you" who used it. Who were you when you used this item? What did you learn through it? What challenges did you face? What obstacles did you overcome? How were you shaped by these experiences?

You may want to change or transform the object, as you are being transformed yourself by becoming married. Honor your apartment or car keys with a new key chain. Block the phone numbers of old beaus. Rip up your Match.com info.

An alternative way to do this ritual is to write words or images describing aspects of your single life that are ending—good and bad—on small slips of paper: Being responsible for every single bill. Leaving the dishes in the sink, unwashed, for three days straight, with no one getting on your case about it. Going to the company Christmas party stag. Sleeping alone. Coming home to an empty house. Breaking up. Being broken up with. Blind dates. First kisses. When you're finished, you may want to burn your pile of papers to symbolize the ending of your single life.

As you handle your single-life items or write on the small slips of paper, be aware of how you feel. Rituals like this often evoke strong emotions, so don't be surprised if you experience feelings of sadness, loss, fear, or anger. Let the feelings wash over you, and reflect on them later by writing in your journal.

You may want to wait to do this exercise a few weeks before your wedding, when you feel fully ready to say good-bye to your single self.

Cold Feet Alert: The "Forever" Questions

 Many brides- and grooms-to-be contact me because they're caught in a vicious circle of asking themselves questions that are simply impossible to answer. Melissa, a twenty-five-year-old MBA student, was one such client.

"All I wanted to do was get engaged," Melissa wrote in an e-mail to me. "Now that I've had this little ring on my finger for two months, I'm having doubts. I just keep wondering: Will we be happy forever? Will we love each other for the next twenty, thirty, fifty years? Or will we get divorced, like my parents did? How can I be guaranteed he's the one for me?"

Before Jack proposed, Melissa had done a kind of cost-benefit analysis on their relationship. Seeing in black and white their strengths and challenges as a couple, as well as his quirks and adorably lovable qualities, Melissa concluded that Jack was indeed Mr. Right-for-Her. Sure, they had their areas of contention, but Melissa was aware of them and ready to accept them. When she thought about having Jack for a husband, she felt lucky; he was a gem.

When Jack proposed, though, it was as if all her pre-engagement analysis got thrown out the window. With the bling on her finger, Melissa started examining their marriage-to-be under a stronger and more powerful microscope. "If I'm having all these questions," she asked, "does that mean there's something wrong? Does it mean I should call off the wedding?"

Not necessarily. As I mentioned in the previous chapter, when you're boyfriend and girlfriend, the idea of a long-term future remains essentially an abstraction. Until he proposed, you probably held yourself back from fully imagining a lifetime together. You were being wisely self-protective. In the back of your mind, you may have worried about the possibility that he'd chicken out, tell you, "I'm not ready," and you'd break up instead. There always existed the slim chance that marriage might not happen.

But now that it's going to happen, the reality of a lifetime with him is settling in. So is the unromantic, scary, and disheartening statistic that about 50 percent of marriages in the United States end in divorce. As a generation, we're painfully aware of this fact, since many of us are, like Melissa, children of divorce who have been affected by the collateral damage a divorce can cause. Plus, we've watched friends fail at "starter" marriages, and we know how sadly commonplace those are, too.

Before Melissa got engaged, the thought of getting divorced from Jack never entered her mind. Now, as she flipped through *Bridal Guide* magazine, she noticed her mind wandering: "Will we love each other *forever*?" Melissa's initial answer—the feeling in her gut—was always yes. But when she tried to examine the question thoroughly, she always ended up getting upset. Her mind raced, her anxiety increased, and her worry that perhaps they weren't the right match intensified. She was stuck in a negative-feedback loop.

The problem is, Melissa was asking questions that are impossible to answer. By wanting the answer to the question "Will we love each other *forever*?" Melissa is trying to look into a crystal ball. She's trying to predict the future. Will they love each other *in thirty years*? Hopefully, but she can't control the challenges life serves up, so this is impossible to answer, too. The same goes for wanting a *guarantee*. By asking herself questions about the far-distant future, Melissa is searching for assurances that do not and cannot exist.

Melissa could continue to make herself batty by asking impossible-to-answer questions like these. Or she could change her own internal dialogue by reframing and rephrasing the questions as more productive ones that relate to the present day. Instead of torturing herself with the unanswerable, "Will we love each other in thirty years?" Melissa needed to ask herself specific questions about her relationship as it existed in the present.

How are we as a couple *today*? Are we interested in and intrigued by each other? Do we support each other's hopes and dreams? Are we supportive of each other? Do we admire each other? Treat each other with respect? When we've faced challenges, how have we done as a couple? Are we a good team, or do we make life more challenging for each other? In arguments, do we shut each other out or do we work to come together? Do we accept each other's differences, or do we try to make each other over in our own images? Are we on the same page about lifestyle, work, family, extended family, money, values, priorities? Do we have chemistry? Love? Passion? Desire? Spice? Do we take good care of each other, or is one the "giver" and one the "givee"?

When Melissa put her future marriage to Jack through these paces by asking frank, present-day questions like these, she was surprised where she landed. "It took a lot of discipline to calm myself down enough to address my cold feet head-on," said Melissa. "But after assessing our relationship up and down, I feel really good. I know in my gut that I'm going to walk down the aisle in a few months with complete confidence about our marriage." For Melissa, taking on her cold feet helped her make an even deeper commitment to her marriage-to-be.

CHAPTER 4

A Family Affair
Leaving Home for Good

Families Behaving Badly

Brides-to-be love to one-up one another with tales of how crazy their family members have started acting since they got engaged. From tales of mothers who hijack the wedding-planning process to fathers who stop talking to the bride-to-be, of older sisters who refuse to wear the pink Nicole Miller bridesmaid dresses to little brothers who are outwardly hostile to the fiancé, crazy family stories can easily fill up hours of discussion in every one of my workshops.

As entertaining as these stories can be, however, bitching and moaning about what's going on does not address the problem. (In fact, it usually gets brides-to-be even more riled up.) So instead, once they've vented about their particular family horror stories, it's my goal to help engaged women understand what's going on beneath the surface—why, for example, they might fight with their mothers about the temperature of the rehearsal dinner lasagna for four months.

The answer, in a nutshell, is quite simple: families behave

badly during the wedding-planning process because their very foundation has become unstable. My dear old dad couldn't have put it better himself as he walked me down the aisle and muttered to me, glumly, "I'm happy to be gaining a son, but I'm sad I'm losing you."

As you prepare to take on your new role of wife, your family inevitably loses some degree of intimacy and time with you. You don't love them any less, of course; you're just redirecting your energies toward your relationship with your husband-to-be, so that the two of you can create the most fulfilling, happiest, healthiest marriage possible.

For many brides-to-be, devoting less time and emotional energy to their families feels like a betrayal, like they're abandoning their families or choosing their fiancés over their families. It's another major change and upheaval that brides-to-be must face, as difficult and complex for some as leaving their single lives.

For Maria, it was especially challenging because she believed that getting married might actually destroy her family.

Wedding-Planning Paralysis

Maria's wedding was five months away, and all she had was her gown. No church or priest. No reception site or caterer. No florist. No photographer. With her September wedding fast approaching, all she had was a poufy white dress and a bundle of nerves.

She'd been engaged to Jeff for over a year—more than enough time to plan a wedding for 150 guests. But Maria felt paralyzed, unable to make even the simplest decisions about the color of table linens or whether to toss her bouquet. At times, Maria felt so stressed that she had difficulty breathing.

"I know it's not cold feet," Maria told a workshop of brides-to-be. "I'm completely confident about Jeff and me, and I can't wait to be married to him.

"What's really weird about this," she continued, "is that I'm a manager at a restaurant, and I'm constantly making decisions. I even occasionally *plan* weddings and formal dinners. This shouldn't be hard for me."

Maria, the oldest of three children, had always been the good girl, the star student, the apple of her parents' eyes. Her brother and sister, six and eight years younger, were far more rebellious than she had ever dared to be. Maria admired their spirits and their willingness to do exactly what they pleased, regardless of their mom and dad's wishes. But at the same time, she sympathized with her parents about how hard it must be to raise these two wild horses.

Maria's parents ran a tight ship when it came to discipline, and when her two siblings became teenagers, all hell broke loose. They skipped classes and missed curfews. Her brother even began to get in trouble with the police.

The family home became a war zone, parents vs. kids, and it fell to Maria to smooth things over between her conservative parents and her wild siblings. "I'm the one everybody talks to," Maria said. "I help everybody get along again." When she lived at home, Maria negotiated peace agreements between the two generations over the dinner table. Now that she was living in Boston, she did diplomacy by cell phone. A few times each week, she'd shut her office door to field irate calls from her parents and siblings ("I know you think Dad's taking your car keys away is unfair," she'd say to her younger brother. "But think about it from Dad's perspective. . . . Wait, is that him yelling at you now? Put Dad on the phone. . . . Dad?") Conversations could go on like that for an hour, the phone being passed from one furious family member to another, each pleading their case to Maria. But Maria never took sides. Her goal was to keep the peace. She was a master at calming everyone down, and she felt like she was the cog that kept her family wheel spinning and not self-destructing.

When Maria started to focus on her wedding shortly after she and Jeff got engaged—and, consequently, to devote a little less time to her role of mediator—tensions at home skyrocketed. The two generations were living under the same roof, but her family members had completely stopped talking to one another.

"No wonder you can't pick up the phone and choose a florist," a bride-to-be interjected. "As soon as you started planning your wedding, your family began to fall apart."

"I hadn't thought of it that way," Maria said. "But you're right—it's so obvious. I can't plan my wedding because deep down I'm wondering, 'What will happen to my family when I get married? Will everyone stop getting along? Will my getting married cause the destruction of my family?'"

For the first time, Maria was able to see her dilemma in stark relief: she couldn't embrace her new life and marriage to Jeff because her family still needed her to be the peacemaker. Putting so much time and energy into helping them prevented her not only from planning her wedding, but also from fully committing to a life, a family, and a future with Jeff, which was what she wanted. Maria loved her family dearly, but she realized that playing peacemaker in a war that had no end was taking too great a toll on her and on her relationship with Jeff.

Maria was at a crossroads. She could stay in her past with her family at the cost of her marriage, or she could move toward her future with Jeff.

Letting Go of Your Family Role

We all play roles within our families of origin; fulfilling our families' needs is one way we get love and attention. In Maria's warring family, for example, someone needed to play the role of peacemaker. Her parents and siblings obviously couldn't do it, since they were the combatants, so she was inevitably cast in the part. Playing that role fulfilled both her need to feel appreciated by each family member and her family's need for a calming presence.

There are an infinite number of roles people play, each dependent on the needs of their particular family. A family that has low energy or has a depressive nature, for example, may need a child to be a spark plug, an instigator, an Energizer bunny. A family that doesn't acknowledge its dysfunction may need a black sheep or scapegoat, someone who can be blamed when things don't go right. A family lacking in structure may need a child who is ultraresponsible, a CEO, a general who keeps them all on track.

We don't consciously choose these roles. Most often, we are cast in them as small children, and throughout our childhoods and young adulthoods we learn to play them to perfection. As adults, however, these roles can become confining and rigid because they express only one aspect of our personalities. As we mature, it's natural to want to expand and grow out of these roles and develop in other, new ways.

Getting married is one of those times when it's necessary to shed some of your old ways so that you can embrace new ways of being. Maria, for example, wanted to be fully and wholeheartedly married to Jeff. She wanted to expand her self-image to include the role of wife. She also wanted to de-emphasize her role as peacemaker. She would always be there for her family in some capacity to offer them love and support, but she was tired of refereeing squabbles and ready to live more for herself and her husband-to-be. She wanted to devote time to building her new, married life and the foundation of her new family. This required a major change not only in her perspective, but in her behavior as well.

To redefine her role within her family, Maria had to first become aware of how easily she slipped into peacemaker mode. Once she started tracking herself, she was amazed at how frequently it happened. Each time a family member called to complain, Maria dropped whatever she had been doing and slipped into high problem-solving gear. Eventually, however, she learned how to create stronger boundaries. When MOM & DAD popped up on her cell phone's screen, she'd say to herself, "I'm not going to be the peacemaker; I'm not going to get overly involved." On those occasions, instead of trying to fix the problems, Maria just listened to her mom rant and rave. Maria actively chose not to get sucked in. She didn't even need to shut her office door since she was simply saying, "Yes, Mom," "I know, Mom," and "That's hard, Mom." Her mom felt heard, which made her feel better, and Maria didn't get overly involved, and that felt great. With her boundaries becoming stronger, Maria wasn't devoting as much emotional energy to her family, and, miraculously, they hadn't killed each other. In fact, with Maria out of the middle, the parents and kids were starting to figure things out for themselves. They learned how to talk directly to one another and not through Maria and, eventually, how to resolve problems—an unexpected turn of events. For Maria, the outcome was even better. As she loosened her ties to her family role of peacemaker, she noticed that she started feeling even closer to Jeff. Instead of spending hours deconstructing her family's latest drama, Maria and Jeff could focus on each other—the life they were building, the family they'd have, the love they shared. They even started planning the wedding—choosing a reception site, putting down deposits on tuxedos, even deciding on lilac as the color of their table linens.

The Emotional To-Do List Item #6
The Role You Play

 In your journal, write about the role you play in your family. Are you the peacemaker, referee, or family counselor? Are you the good girl, the quiet one, the helpful child? Or are you the rebel, the black sheep, the rascal? Are you your mom's confidante or your dad's best friend?

How does your playing this role help your family? How does it keep the family functioning?

How does playing that role help you? How does it fulfill your need for appreciation and affection? How does it give you power or influence in your family? Also, how does it limit you? What aspects of your personality don't get expressed when you play your family role?

How does your role affect your marriage-to-be? Can you continue to play your old role and still create the foundation of a good marriage with your husband-to-be, or does your family role limit how much you can give to your relationship with him?

Imagine what it would be like if you spent less time playing your family role and devoting more time to the family you'll be creating with your husband. How will your marriage benefit? What power and influence in your family will you have to give up?

The Final Cut of the Apron Strings

Brides-to-be who have extremely close relationships with family members often feel conflicted during their engagements. They simultaneously want to stay in the comfort and familiarity of their families and fall into the warm, welcoming arms of their fiancés. Rachel, who had the meltdown in the yo-

gurt aisle days after getting engaged, experienced these ambivalent feelings when it came to her relationship with her dad.

Rachel had left her childhood home at age eighteen to go
to college, and she hadn't lived there since. Although she still
lived in the same city as her parents, Rachel was busy with
her career as a systems analyst, her social life, and endless
fixer-upper jobs on her condo, so the only time Rachel saw
them was at their weekly Sunday suppers.

As her mom tended the roast, Rachel and her dad would
go for walks or sit by the fire and talk. She shared with him
the latest developments at work and her problems with the
plumbers, seeking his advice and input on everything that
was happening in her life. "He's always been my rock, my
calming force," Rachel told a workshop of brides-to-be. "Especially when I was single. When I didn't have a boyfriend,
he was the main man in my life." Her dad, meanwhile, was
far more dependent on Rachel for his emotional sustenance.
He talked to Rachel about his transition into retirement and
his struggles with how to fill his days and feel like a productive human being. They gossiped about the family—aunts
and uncles and her two older brothers, who had moved thousands of miles away. "My mom calls us the 'two peas in a
pod,'" she said.

When her fiancé Dave suggested with excitement that
they carry on her family's tradition and begin having their
own special Sunday suppers, Rachel was torn. On the one
hand, she was touched that Dave was thinking about ways
that they could start new family traditions. It made her excited and happy about her future with such a considerate,

sweet guy. And she really loved the idea of adopting the Sunday supper tradition for their own new family. On the other hand, she was sad for her dad. "I'm the only one who really understands him, and he counts on my visit every week," she explained. "My mom's a great person, but she's not very emotional, so my dad stores up everything he needs to talk about and shares it with me on Sundays. What's he going to do without me?" The following weekend, Rachel stopped by her parents' house in the early afternoon so that she could get home to Dave and their first Sunday supper together.

"When I announced that I had to get going, my dad started stuttering, 'Oh. Oh. Okay," Rachel told the workshop, choking up with tears as she recounted that day. "I knew what his 'Oh. Okay,' meant: it meant that he was hurt and trying not to show it."

As Rachel pulled out of the driveway, her dad gave her a slow, sad wave. "I made it about two blocks before I had to pull over because I was crying so hard," she said. "It hurt me so much to be hurting him. At the same time, I really wanted to start the tradition with Dave. The whole thing tore me up!"

Many brides-to-be feel divided like this: between taking care of their parents the way they always have and maintaining the same degree of closeness that they've always had, and wanting to devote more energy to their relationship with their fiancé. And it's not just dads and daughters who face this problem. It happens with mothers, too—especially for those brides-to-be who consider their mom to be their best friend. The point is, when you have an extremely close relationship with a parent (or a sibling, but we'll get to that later in this chapter), the intimacy and connectedness between you that feels so good and comfortable can become an obstacle to deepening your relationship with your fiancé.

This is one of the hardest realities that brides-to-be have to face, but in order to develop healthy and intimate relationships with other people, you have to let go of some of the closeness that you have with your parents. The whole course of your development as an individual—from the moment you were born—consists of a series of tiny steps out of the arms of your parents and into the wider world. It's difficult and it's sad, but it's necessary. As long as you remain primarily your parents' child—even by acting as their best friend—you're not available to give yourself fully to a relationship with your significant other or with any children you may have in the future.

Since loosening your ties to your parents can be a painful process for them and you, during your engagement, the separation often gets played out through small slights and rejections, misunderstandings and missteps. Rachel's dad, for example, had always been a gusher, quick with compliments and effusive praise whenever Rachel dressed up, be it for church or prom or even their Sunday dinners. When she modeled her wedding dress for him, however, he went mute. "There I was, wearing the most beautiful dress I'd ever wear for the most important day of my life, and my dad just stared at me blankly," she recalled. "He had nothing to say. No reaction. No comment. He just nodded and walked out of the room, stone-faced. It broke my heart."

This scenario repeated itself again and again throughout her engagement. Whenever the wedding was discussed,

Rachel's dad closed down. She could feel him pulling away and shutting her out. "This just seems to be really painful for both of us," she said. "I feel like I'm losing my biggest supporter, my loudest cheerleader, and he feels like he's losing the one person in the world who really understands him."

Normally, Rachel and her dad would talk through conflicts like this, but with her wedding fast approaching, talking about the tensions seemed taboo; the myth that engagement is supposed to be only a happy time strikes again.

What Rachel needed to do was talk to her dad. By openly discussing what was going on between them—letting him know that devoting less time and energy to him was breaking her heart as much as it was his, but that she felt that she *needed* to do it for the health of her marriage-to-be—there was a good chance that the two peas in a pod could work through it together instead of passive-aggressively hurting and being hurt, as they both were during the wedding-dress incident.

One Sunday afternoon, Rachel pulled her dad aside. It was scary to bring up the tension between them, but she plunged right in. "I feel like I'm abandoning you, Dad," Rachel said. "It's killing me to be spending less time with you, but I know that I have to, for my marriage, and for me, to be able to fully transition from my old life into my new one. It doesn't mean I love you any less; it just means that Dave's got to become my main man."

"I know, honey," her dad replied. "I know."

Their talk went well and Rachel felt closer to her dad—he wasn't nearly as standoffish anymore—but Rachel still dreaded the walk down the aisle with him; she couldn't bear

the thought of letting him go. As they took their first steps together, however, she found that she was overwhelmed with
excitement. "It was amazing!" she wrote in an e-mail to me
after the wedding. "Seeing my fiancé at the end of the aisle
and seeing the church decorated for us was just great!

"The next five steps we took, however, I became filled
with sadness," she went on. "We were approaching *the* moment my dad was to give me away, and it was almost unbear-
able. My eyes welled up with tears, and for a moment, I
wanted time to stand still."

Rachel had predicted that her dad would be a weepy mess
all the way down the aisle, but on that important walk, she noticed that something had changed in him. No longer was he
looking and acting like a hurt little puppy, as he had for much
of her engagement. As he walked her down the aisle, he was
steady, calm, and strong. "At that moment, I realized that he
was really proud of me and proud of the woman I had become," she wrote. "He was happy I had found this wonderful
guy. And he was ready to let me go. He was really okay."

The final five steps down the aisle were "absolute joy," she
said. "When we met my fiancé at the altar, my dad said to
him, 'Take care of her, Dave. Hug her and tell her that you
love her every single day — maybe even twice a day.' My father had done these things for me every day of my life, and he
was handing over this responsibility and honor to Dave. It
was a gesture of love and trust, as well as a 'Take good care
of my little girl' message."

The men shook hands, and her dad joined her mom in the
pew. "The walk was so intense," she said. "I reexperienced

every single emotion I had felt during the engagement — all in thirty seconds!"

Saying the vows, she said, was simply wonderful. "I had made a long journey through the engagement process, and the vows were my prize at the end," she said. "I was so proud that I had let go of some of my closeness with and dependence on my dad, and I was so proud to be marrying this fabulous man."

There's no way Rachel could have foreseen, on that sad Sunday afternoon when she pulled out of her parents' driveway, that ending her role as her dad's closest confidante could have such a positive outcome. But on her wedding day, as she and Dave danced their first dance, out of the corner of her eye she could see her father, beaming with pride and delight. Everyone was just fine.

Becoming a Peer

One way to see what's happening emotionally within your family is to draw your genogram — or, as I call it, your family map. Family maps are similar to family trees, but they express the emotional relationships within a family, not genealogy. If you are extremely close to your mother and one sister, for example, but you don't have any contact whatsoever with your father and a contentious relationship with your brother, all that information can be depicted in your family map. Seeing the relationships pictorially may help you see the issues going on within your family more clearly.

When Jasmine saw her family map take shape during a

workshop for brides-to-be, she was able to understand the various dynamics at work, as well as what she needed to do to change them. She had contacted me midway through her engagement because she was having problems with her older sister.

Days after Tim proposed to Jasmine, Bethany jumped on a plane to help her little sister start planning the wedding. "Tim was shocked at how passive I became around my sister," Jasmine told the workshop. "Bethany showed up on our doorstep with stacks of bridal magazines and a long list of things we needed to accomplish while she was in town. Tim kept pulling me aside and saying, 'Hey, we haven't discussed anything about our wedding yet. Why are you letting her make decisions for us?'" During Bethany's visit, Tim got to know a whole new side of Jasmine that he had never seen before: the flaky little sister.

The household Jasmine and Bethany grew up in was deeply unhappy. Their parents were married, but just barely. They were true 'til-death-do-you-part people, still chugging along after several decades despite their constant fighting, nagging, and name-calling. To compensate for the unhappy family they were growing up in, Bethany and Jasmine had created a happy mini family of just the two of them. As little girls, Bethany, the older sister, was the mommy, and Jasmine was the baby.

Their mother-daughter relationship continued once they grew up and moved out of their house, even though both "Mommy" and "Baby" were adult women. Whenever Jasmine moved into a new apartment, for example, Bethany would fly in to help her little sister get organized. The sisters were extremely close, and through the years they had forged a tight bond.

As the brides-to-be in my workshops tell their family stories, I stand at a white board and draw their family maps to depict the emotional relationships within the family. In Jasmine's family map, her parents' rocky relationship is indicated with a jagged line (vvv). Bethany and Jasmine's balanced relationships with each parent (not too close, not too rocky) are each marked with one solid line (|). The two sisters' unbalanced and unhealthily close relationship is marked with two lines (||).

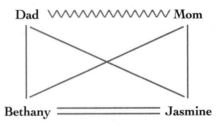

In an ideal world, every relationship between every family member would be marked by one solid line (|), signifying that the relationship is healthy and flexible enough to allow for connectedness and intimacy as well as separation and individuality. (Bethany and Jasmine had these types of relationships with both parents.) But families are often messy, complex, and all too human. Indeed, in most families, there are usually a number of either unhealthily close or too-distant relationships.

In Jasmine's case, her relationship with her sister—who was only two years older than she—was more a parent-child relationship than a sibling relationship. I redrew Jasmine's family map to reflect more accurately the parent-child nature of her relationship with her sister, and for Jasmine, seeing this brought the issue into focus:

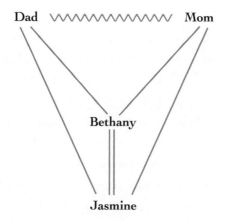

When Jasmine saw herself in the "baby" position in the family map, not only was she embarrassed to be seen that way by the other brides-to-be, she was also angry with herself. "That's definitely not who I am," she commented. "I'm not a baby in any other relationship. It's only with Bethany, and that's gotta stop." It was time, Jasmine believed, to grow up and out of the little-sister role and to become a peer with her sister. Jasmine had had enough of being the baby to Bethany's all-knowing mother hen.

"At the beginning of our engagement, I let Bethany take over the wedding planning because it was hard for me to tell her, 'Hey, this is my wedding, and this is how I want it,'" Jasmine recounted during a phone call a few months after the workshop. "I'd never stood up to her like that before. I always went along. But I realized that I didn't want to be that way anymore. I was tired of being the helpless little girl with her."

Jasmine knew that she had to change her behavior, but before she could, she had to examine the part *she* played in perpetuating the mother-daughter relationship. She had to look at how and why, for example, she agreed to let her sister fly in to help her unpack her apartment when she was perfectly capable of doing it herself. Jasmine had to become aware of how often she acquiesced to her sister's desires at the expense of her own, just to keep the peace between them — how, for example, she went along with all the bridal-shop appointments Bethany had set up instead of saying what she really felt, which was, "Hey, I'm not ready to try on wedding dresses!" In essence, Jasmine had to plug in to her needs and desires, and not just cave to Bethany's.

"My sister and I got into a huge spat over the bouquets," she told me during our phone call. "She thought the nosegay I wanted was too informal for the tone of the wedding, and she kept pushing for a formal cascading bouquet. But when I stuck to my guns, she got really mad at me, furious. She didn't talk to me for a few days. I got really anxious — that I had hurt her feelings, that I had damaged our relationship. I almost started hyperventilating, I was so upset."

Planning Jasmine's wedding was a time of high drama for

the two sisters. "Every time I said, 'Tim and I have something else in mind,' to one of Bethany's suggestions for the menu, shoes, or decorations, Bethany would stop speaking to me for a few days," remembered Jasmine. "I know it sounds like she was being petulant, but I didn't take it that way. I think it shocked her when I didn't agree with her. She had to disappear for a few days to come to terms with what was happening."

Jasmine, meanwhile, had to learn how to tolerate her own anxiety about her sister's reactions. She had to learn to live with the fact that what she was doing was hurting her sister. She had to watch Bethany be confused, and not save her from her pain. As she and Tim planned their wedding their way, Jasmine began to step out of her comfortable role as the baby sister and fully into her life as a competent woman, even in her relationship with her sister.

Bethany responded in kind. "It was rough at first," remembered Jasmine. "But the more confident I became in myself and in my decisions, the more Bethany saw me as a grown, adult, capable woman. She stopped being my mother hen, and she started being my sister."

Through the planning of the wedding, Jasmine and Bethany were able to forge a new relationship as sisters. Every little disagreement and squabble helped them rework their relationship and create a new relationship as peers. No longer domineering mother and flaky child, Bethany and Jasmine were two separate, adult sisters who could love each other and support each other. They were equals.

Meanwhile, as Jasmine loosened her ties to Bethany, she was able to invest more time, love, and energy into the new

Jasmine-and-Tim family. (In the family map below, her overly close—double-line—relationship with Bethany has been replaced by the healthier single line.) She and Bethany continue to be close—best friends, even—but Jasmine's primary family bond is now with Tim, her husband-to-be, as it should be.

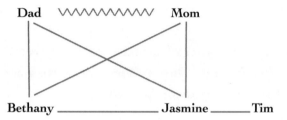

The Emotional To-Do List Item #7
Drawing Your Family Map

Drawing your family map and seeing the emotional relationships within your family laid out in black and white can help you become aware of the emotional work you may need to do during your engagement.

1. To begin, write down all the members in your family by generation, in the style of a family tree.

2. Next, draw your emotional relationships with your family members. For example, if you have a healthy, emotionally balanced relationship with your father that allows for connectedness and intimacy as well as separation and individuality, indicate that with a single line (I). If you're extremely (perhaps unhealthily)

close to your mother, mark that with a double line (II). If you have a rocky relationship with a sibling, use a jagged line (vvv). If you don't have a relationship with your father, indicate the cutoff with a broken line (- - - -).

3. Next, draw all other family relationships, including healthy, overly close, difficult, and cutoff relationships.

4. Now step back and look at your family map. With whom are you overly close and entwined? With whom are you distant? What role do you play in your family? How has your role affected your relationships and your ability to be fully "in" your relationship with your fiancé?

5. Finally, draw your fiancé into your family map. Use one single line (I) to represent your (hopefully) emotionally balanced and healthy relationship. Reflect on the impact of his joining your family on your family members and your relationships with them. Might your mother or father feel replaced by him? How do you think your siblings are reacting to this new guy in the family?

Your family map can be a powerful tool for your own personal growth. As you loosen your ties to your family of origin so you can form a strong bond with your husband-to-be, observe how your relationships change—how the lines in the map take different shapes—as you continue to do your work.

Regrieving the Death of a Parent

Brides-to-be who have lost a parent may find themselves feeling the loss even more powerfully during their engagement—sometimes on a whole new level. The searing pain of grief is often accompanied by anger at the dead parent—anger that he or she isn't here to celebrate their marriage, anger at being abandoned by their parent, anger that their engagement has a cloud of grief and loss hanging over it.

For Tracy, whose mother passed away three years before her wedding, bridal salons were painful triggers for her grief. "All those mothers and daughters shopping for dresses together broke my heart," she told me. "I brought my maid of honor shopping with me, but it wasn't the same. I wanted my mom to be with me, and she wasn't."

Saleswomen in the bridal shops unwittingly poured salt into her wounds when they asked her, "Where's your mom?" and "Would you like to bring your mother in to see the dress?"

"I never got up the nerve to say, 'She's dead,' to point out how thoughtless their comments were, but I wanted to," remembered Tracy. "Instead, I'd end up slinking out of the bridal shop feeling embarrassed, exposed, and sad. And angry at my mom, too, for putting me through this, for leaving me to do this by myself. I hated buying my dress, shoes, and veil. It was just too painful."

Tracy's sister-in-law had been through the same thing; she'd married Tracy's brother just six months after her own mother's death. Her compassion turned out to be a great help to Tracy. "I randomly called her up to tell her I was missing my mom," said Tracy. "We'd cry on the phone together about our moms. She grieved with me, and she completely understood. She didn't try to make the pain go away or make it 'better.' And, on the bright side, it ended up bonding us a lot closer."

The week of her wedding, an old family friend stopped by

Tracy's house to drop off a wedding gift. "This friend is a social worker, and she's very in tune, very in touch, with others," said Tracy. "She looked at me compassionately and said, 'I can't imagine how hard getting married must be, not having a mom.' When she acknowledged my situation like that, all my walls and all my defenses came tumbling down. More so, even, than with my sister-in-law because I was always a bit worried I'd go too far and upset her too much. But with my friend, I could be really upset, and she was fine with it."

After her friend left, Tracy threw herself on the bed and sobbed for an hour. "I cried and let it all out," she remembered. "I felt angry at the unfairness, angry at my mom for leaving. I felt raw, heartbroken, and sad." The grief walloped her, beat her up. "I didn't fight it because I knew it was important to feel," she continued. "I wanted to feel the grief so that it would move on and not overwhelm me later."

On the day of her wedding, Tracy woke up feeling a little sad, missing her mom. As she went about her business, though—the hair, the makeup, the dress—she started to become more excited. As the day progressed, the air became thick with humidity. "It was incredibly hot," she remembered. "And I started worrying about my guests being hot and sticky, my curly hair frizzing out, and my face being sweaty."

As the limo drove her to the church, Tracy fingered her mom's rosary, and a pit of sadness opened up in her stomach once again. Then, on top of that, it started to rain.

When Tracy stepped out of the limo at the church, however, the showers stopped, the humidity broke, and the sun came out. "It ended up being a perfect day," said Tracy. "The sun, the temperature, the clear, clean air—that's how I knew my mom was there for me. As I got out of the limo and walked toward the church, I felt connected to her through the beautiful day she brought me."

Tracy had planned to honor her mother's memory with a symbolic rose ceremony during her wedding. "But as soon as I arrived at the church, I almost canceled it," she remembered. "I was already feeling so connected to my mom. I could feel people thinking about her, missing her, and loving her. We ended up doing the rose ceremony, but I didn't need it to feel her love. I could feel her with me all day long. I knew she was there."

Cold Feet Alert: Unraveling the Old Knot Before Tying the New One

 Sometimes cold feet can look like cold feet, but they're not actually cold feet, in the negative, I-need-to-call-off-my-wedding sense. Instead, they're feelings about an old, unresolved issue in your life. Diana's story is a classic example of how misleading cold feet can initially be.

Knots in her stomach kept Diana awake for the entire first week after Kyle proposed. "I tossed and turned, wondering, 'If I'm newly engaged and doubled over in pain, is getting married to him really what's best for me and my happiness?'" she told me.

As she tossed and turned, Diana created checklists in her mind to make sure they were a good match: "Do I love him? Yes.

Is there a lot of passion between us? Yes. Do we have similar dreams and goals? Yes."

Her anxiety didn't abate, so she turned to her journal to write a "Why I Love Kyle" list: *He's passionate about life. He's responsible. He's a man of the world. He's good with people. He's an architect. He's an artist. He's creative. He looks at the world differently from me. He's kidlike. He admits when he's wrong. He listens. He's supportive. He's affectionate. He's thoughtful. He really loves me. He's attractive. He's sexy. His mind fascinates me.*

Her "What I Don't Love About Kyle" list was short: *He can be moody. He's very private. He plays a lot of golf. He can be quiet and shy in social situations. He hates big gatherings, while I love them; I'm much more social and extroverted than he is.*

Reading her lists side by side, Diana saw that she wasn't ambivalent about her fiancé; she loved him deeply. She admired him, and she was intrigued by him. Yes, she foresaw that his need for solitude and her need for socializing would challenge them as a couple, but it was hardly a deal-breaker, and certainly no reason for her to call off the wedding. Yet her panicky feelings and knotted-up stomach remained. What was going on?

"On your Web site," she said to me, "I read that cold feet can be due to the relationship *or* to a past event in my life. That's when a lightbulb went off: my parents' divorce is the real source of my cold feet."

When Diana's parents had divorced ten years earlier, it had been a huge relief. They'd been making each other and the entire family miserable for years, and their divorce was the end of a long, unhappy chapter in her family's history.

Days after Diana got engaged, however, the legacy of her parents' toxic marriage reared its head, manifesting and masquerading as a case of cold feet. "I instantly attached the fear I was feeling to marrying Kyle," she said. "But what I'm really afraid of is that I'm ill-equipped for marriage." Diana feared that she didn't know what a happy, healthy, long-lasting marriage really looked like, and she was scared that she might be destined to fail.

The more Diana and I explored her fears of failure, the more painful memories of how cruelly her parents had treated each other began to surface. She felt sadness and despair about how much her parents fought, how they lived in misery for so long, and how she had been so affected and hurt by it all—emotions and thoughts she'd never let herself feel before.

On the threshold of marriage, it wasn't much of a surprise that Diana had to revisit these old wounds. But feeling the grief wasn't easy for her. For a while, her pain even increased, but gradually the emotions started to change into acceptance: "Once I understood that my anxiety wasn't about Kyle," she said, "the painful emotions became more bearable. I had no idea that I'd be going backward in time to reopen the wounds of my parents' divorce, but it was clearly where I needed to go, emotionally."

Ironically, the sadder Diana felt about her family, the happier and more confident she felt about marrying Kyle. "It's strange, but as I processed my feelings about my parents' divorce at such a deep level, I became even more grateful that I'm marrying Kyle," she said. "It's helped me see that I've got this incredible opportunity to start a new, happier, healthier family with him." By giving in to her grief about her past, Diana was able to embrace her future with Kyle happily and wholeheartedly.

CHAPTER 5

From "Me" to "We"
The Private Life of Engaged Couples

Different from Dating

I probably don't need to tell you that there are benefits galore to being engaged. On the most superficial level, there's that gorgeous ring on your left hand, and the excitement of announcing your engagement to the world, followed by the parties thrown in your honor and the loads of presents that arrive on your doorstep.

On a deeper level, as you and your fiancé loosen your ties to your single lives and your families of origin, you also begin to entwine your lives more permanently. You're planning your wedding, building your nest, playing with names for your future kids, and perhaps envisioning yourselves gray-haired, shuffling hand in hand through your retirement together. Best of all, now that you're engaged, you're free to think in terms of "the rest of my life." That's a train of thought you likely didn't let yourself get on when you were just dating. Now that you're here, though, you can sit back and relax into the security of your future as a family (of two, four, or six!) stretching out before you.

And yet, getting engaged can also shock even the happiest couples' system. After all, overnight, you have catapulted from the unofficial and largely unrecognized status of boy-friend and girlfriend into what will result in the new realm of the state-sanctioned married couple—and this change in legal status can impact the tone and intensity of your everyday life. Bride-to-be Pauline felt it right away. "As soon as we got engaged, my mind-set went from, 'He's great, and this relationship is fun,' to 'Wow, this is the rest of our lives,'" she told me. "That phrase had never crossed my mind when we were dating. But soon it became a soundtrack playing in my head, Muzak that would sometimes make me ecstatic and sometimes make me scared."

Many engaged couples feel like their relationships become public property once the engagement is announced. When happy well-wishers throw parties for you, all eyes are on the two of you from the moment you walk through the door, observing your every interaction with each other, seeing how you fit together and whether you're a good match. (Not that it's their business, but people just can't seem to stop themselves.) As an engaged couple, it's likely that you sometimes feel like goldfish in a bowl.

Being thrust into the limelight can be stressful enough, but what happens when real life intervenes? Just because you're planning a wedding doesn't mean the world screeches to a halt. During your engagement, you may face money problems when the renovations on the new house you and your fiancé just bought run way over budget; one of you may have job stress when a promotion requires you or your fiancé to spend days, nights, and weekends at work; or health crises may come your way when a family member gets sick. Sometimes bad things happen, even to engaged people.

Shawna's fiancé, Jim, was laid off from his job three weeks after he proposed. "Not only was Jim worried about finding a new job," she told me, "but he felt totally humiliated and insecure about going to all these parties after the layoff, too."

"Your dad's friends are going to ask me what I do for a living," Jim would say to her. "What am I going to tell them? 'Well, sir, I'm unemployed, and no, I can't give her the lifestyle she's accustomed to?'" Shawna felt terrible for Jim. It broke her heart that he was going through this, especially during their engagement. "And to tell you the truth," she admitted, "I was a little embarrassed about the layoff, too."

When they attended engagement parties, however, Shawna and Jim put on their best game faces. "We deserve an Oscar!" Shawna said. "We played the role of the perfectly untroubled engaged couple so well. We couldn't let anyone see our stress because we didn't want them to question our getting married. It was tough."

Tensions often rise inside an engaged couple's fishbowl. In fact, most brides-to-be tell me that during their engagements, they fight more, have less sex, feel less close, and spend a lot of time evaluating and analyzing their relationship. To find out how true this was, I took a survey. I asked each bride I interviewed for this book, "Since your engagement, your relationship with your fiancé has":

A. *Flourished. We feel more connected and more deeply in love every day. Wedding planning has been a breeze, and this is one of the happiest times of our lives thus far.*

B. *Had its ups and downs. Being engaged has been more challenging than we expected and we're hitting some bumps in the road, but overall we're dealing with it pretty well.*

C. *Been really challenging. We're feeling less connected to each other, and there's much more tension between us. The state of our relationship concerns us both.*

The Emotional To-Do List Item #8
What's Your Answer?

 Before you read the results, how would you answer this question? Has your relationship flourished? Had its ups and downs? Been really challenging? Take a moment to assess the state of your relationship since you got engaged. You may even want to ask your fiancé what he thinks.

Now for the answers to this survey, which may both relieve and astound you.

Only 20 percent of the people responding said their relationship had flourished. "Before we were engaged, there was always that sense that either of us could get out of the relationship if the going got tough," one bride-to-be said. "But now we know we're here to stay, and we'll work things out no matter what." Another reported: "We both feel ourselves deepening into the relationship. Now it's more than just infatuation and love. It's forever, and that feels great." In short, this minority felt like their engagement was in fact the happiest time of their lives.

A full 50 percent of respondents said their relationships were up and down. "How can it not be?" said one bride-to-be. "Your families are officially involved in your relationship!" Said another: "We had some real lows, and whenever we argued both of us would get riddled with doubts. But the last third of our engagement (thank God for long engagements!) we were happy, connected, and excited."

Finally, 30 percent said being engaged was a challenge. "Suddenly, we had to make unanimous decisions on everything, and we ended up fighting about almost all of it," said one bride-to-be. Said another: "It's been hard to keep things stable between us emotionally because we both have so many emotions going on at once—individually and together. It's just been really stressful."

Pull back the curtain on the relationship of an engaged couple and what do you see? Two individuals getting to know each other on a whole new, deeper level.

Planning a Wedding . . . Together

The most obvious external factor that causes engagement to be an up-and-down time for couples is the wedding itself. Planning your perfect wedding—for you as an individual— would likely be a piece of cake. You know your own style (elegant vs. casual), priorities (flowers trump favors), and finances (your parents' bankroll or your own Visa credit limit). Planning the perfect wedding for you as a *couple*, however, is a different matter. It's impossible for you and your fiancé to have perfectly in-sync images and fantasies about your wedding because you're different people with different backgrounds and different ideas about what makes a wedding perfect. Still, you have to hammer out a compromise that makes both of you reasonably happy.

Phoebe and Carl had been living together for three years before they got engaged, so she assumed planning their wedding would be a breeze. They'd successfully negotiated the little things of day-to-day life—who paid the bills, who cooked, who cleaned. They loved each other, and they were a good team.

Three months before the wedding, Phoebe was overwhelmed with all that was still left to do. "I said to Carl, 'We need to divvy up the tasks,'" she told me. "'You write your list, and I'll write mine.'"

Carl's list was short and sweet, about four or five items, including "Buy gifts for ushers," "Hire band," and "Order wine." Phoebe's list was, shall we say, a tad more detailed:

1. ORDER WINE

   a. Go to wine store.
   b. Discuss options with wine man. Buy a few bottles to try out.
   c. Taste test.
   d. Decide on wine.
   e. Determine how many glasses per person.
   f. Purchase wine.

    g. Arrange for wine to be delivered to wedding site.

    h. Fax map and directions.

    i. Arrange for tarp to be put over wine.

2. HIRE BAND

    a. Buy twelve CDs from local bands.

    b. Choose band.

    c. Hire band—do contracts, etc.

    d. Fax map and directions.

    e. Ask: Does band need to change clothes?

    f. Ask: Does band need to eat?

    g. Determine where will band change and eat.

When they compared lists, Carl blew up. "Phoebe, I just want this to be a big party, not an uptight, scheduled thing," he said. "I want all my friends to be able to pull up a chair and talk."

"That's what I want, too!" Phoebe replied. "But I also want there to be a chair for them to pull up!"

For his part, Carl thought he was more involved with the wedding than the average guy. Every night over dinner, he listened to Phoebe's latest brainstorm about the favors, and he gave his two cents' worth on every decision from food to flowers. "I think I'm being a really good guy, here," he said. "Just because I wrote 'Hire band' instead of a fifteen-point plan doesn't mean I don't know what needs to be done. I know we need to do contracts. I know we need to fax directions. I just don't write it all down the way you do."

Phoebe listened and gave Carl the impression that she was

fine. She knew he'd never thrown a party fancier than a backyard barbeque, so no wonder Mr. Naive thought he could keep all the details in his head. He'd never picked up a bridal magazine or laid eyes on a party planner's to-do list before, so he didn't have a clue what was involved in pulling off their wedding.

Privately, however, Phoebe fumed and felt she wasn't getting the help she needed. The responsibility of the wedding was still, she thought, solely on her shoulders, and she didn't want to carry the burden — or the stress — alone. She felt like she was drowning in details.

Why didn't she make her needs clear? "I'd waited three years for him to propose, and I wanted to get married so badly that I didn't want to rock the boat at all," she said. "I was afraid I'd scare him off if I asked him for more help or showed him that I wasn't a hundred percent pulled together. So I kept trying to control all the wedding details so that I didn't have to deal with the emotional crap that was going on."

But the "emotional crap," as she called it, can't be avoided. In a way, a wedding is an ideal vehicle for an engaged couple to learn how to work together. It forces you to see each other for who you really are. As you make a series of binding and expensive decisions together about who, what, where, when, and how much, you see firsthand each other's strengths and weaknesses in a way you probably haven't before. It brings to the surface your differences — in personalities, priorities, methodology, organization, and values. Spending vast amounts of money in a brief window of time on an event that holds so much symbolic value and importance to you is a major test of your relationship.

Phoebe and Carl failed that test, essentially, because Phoebe stifled her need for help, and Carl assumed he was doing enough because Phoebe never made a peep to the contrary. "If I'm honest with myself, I spent a huge amount of our engagement furious with Carl," Phoebe told me three years after their wedding. "It wasn't good."

Their dysfunctional dynamic came to a head soon after their first wedding anniversary when their daughter was born. "I was still afraid to tell him I needed to go to bed at nine P.M. because I'd have to get up to feed the baby at eleven thirty P.M., one A.M., three A.M., and five A.M.," she said.

It wasn't until their daughter was six weeks old and Phoebe fell apart in exhaustion that they thrashed it out. In the middle of the night, with a screaming infant in her arms, Phoebe's resentments—going all the way back to the wedding planning—came spilling out. "Carl had no idea that I was hanging on to so much anger that he didn't do enough to help me with the wedding, with the baby, or even with little things like buying milk and bread and making sure we had toothpaste in the house," she said. "How could he? I never let on that I was mad, or that I needed more from him. Carl felt ambushed and attacked by my outburst, and he got mad right back at me, and he was perfectly justified."

Sleep deprived, with an infant to care for and eighteen months of resentment built up, Phoebe and Carl wisely realized that they didn't have the skills or the wherewithal to fix this problem themselves. They'd dug themselves into a hole, and they needed some help digging themselves out, so off to a couples' counselor they went. In that safe atmosphere, Phoebe was finally able to express the pain, insecurity, and anger of having to wait for three years for Carl to be as ready for marriage as she was. They'd never broached the subject before—it was too hot—and it was at the heart of why Phoebe felt she always had to strive for perfection. With new awareness of each other, they were able to abandon their old dynamic, which had been set up during the wedding-planning process of Phoebe putting on an "I don't need help" face and Carl taking her at, well, face value, and replace it with open communication and clear expectations. As a result, their team—their marriage—became genuinely strong.

If I Knew *Then* What I Know *Now* . . .
He Didn't Care About Our Forks

I thought that because it was *our* wedding, we should decide every single little thing together, and I got frustrated with Ben when he didn't share my enthusiasm for the really small details.

One day, we went to register. We had fun for a while, shooting pots and pans with the scanner gun. But then we had to choose china and silverware, and he couldn't have cared less. He got impatient with my comparing patterns and designs, and he got a little bratty, too. It all came to a head when I showed him different forks.

"Do you really care about this stuff?" he scoffed.

"No," I lied. I was having a ball choosing flatware, but I censored my enthusiasm. "But we need to put something on the list so we don't get forks we hate."

The whole episode pissed me off, so later that day I called a girlfriend to complain about the guy I was going to marry. Thank God for girlfriends! She gave me a whole new perspective on the fork fiasco.

"Ben feels the same way about forks," she said to me, "as you do about buying the latest DVD player or PalmPilot. He couldn't care less, but that has no bearing on his interest in your relationship, wedding, or marriage."

To paraphrase Freud, sometimes a fork is just a fork. My girlfriend opened my eyes to this, and she and I made a date to go look at forks together. It was much more fun that way.

—Kylie, married one month

Getting Real with Each Other

It may seem counterintuitive, but what Phoebe needed to do during their engagement was show Carl her cracks. She needed to let him know that she wasn't perfect, and that she needed his help and understanding. She needed to be her real, messy self during their engagement.

Unlike the false front that Phoebe put up, for many couples, engagement is surprisingly similar to MTV's *Real World*—"when people stop being polite and start getting real." And this is a good thing. It's easier to deal with your differences now than it may be three years down the road, when you've got a screaming infant in your arms.

You may be finding that with a ring on your finger, it's as if you've swallowed a truth serum. For example, now that you're engaged, you may finally admit that you hate it when your fiancé's dog sleeps in bed with you at night. Or you may, one evening, announce to him that you really wish that he would wash his own dinner plate—or maybe even cook his own dinner—for once, instead of relying on you to do it every night. Your fiancé will probably be flabbergasted and hurt by these comments, since before you got engaged, you seemed just fine having Rover snuggling between you, and you offered to cook him dinner and wash his plate (and occasional pair of boxer shorts) out of what seemed to be a gesture of love. (More on the pressure engaged and newly married women feel to adopt "wifely duties" such as cooking and cleaning in chapter 9.) For many engaged couples, their true selves make multiple grand entrances like this throughout their engagement.

At the same time that you're showing and seeing these perhaps less-than-lovely new sides of each other, however, you're also likely loving each other more deeply. You're becoming more committed to each other than you've ever been. You're consciously choosing each other 'til death do you part; the exit light over the door has been extinguished. You don't want to walk out, so you have to learn how to work through your problems and differences. For many couples, engagement is a time of great adjustment, as you learn to live with each other and love each other, warts and all.

Dueling Through Differences

As they prepared to move in together, Cynthia and Brian, who got engaged in Alaska among the bears, realized they needed a new couch. There was no way Cynthia was letting Brian's ratty frat-house sofa into her apartment. One Sunday morning about five months before their wedding, they went to the furniture department at Macy's.

"Cynthia, come look at this one!" Brian yelled to her across the floor. Cynthia found him lying down on a sleek, minimalist, black leather couch. "I love it, don't you?" he asked her, a big smile on his face.

"You do?" Cynthia said. To her, the couch looked like it was straight out of a catalog of high-end Italian design. It couldn't be more different than what she had her heart set on. Her design aesthetic leaned toward shabby chic, and she had an overstuffed floral couch with lots of pillows in mind. She wanted something to sink into, not some hard, black leather monstrosity.

They clashed over their different design aesthetics for weeks. Each tried to persuade, cajole, or guilt-trip the other into giving in, but neither would budge. At times, they even ridiculed the other's choices—the words "S&M School of Design" and "tacky girlishness" crossed their lips. These comments hurt.

Even couples who think they've covered all the essential topics before getting engaged are often broadsided by the differences that emerge once the "rest of my life" soundtrack switches on. She's a huge environmentalist; he's not really that passionate about recycling. He feels a much greater pull to his Jewish roots than he expected; she thought the no-religion decision was final. He likes crunchy peanut butter; she likes creamy. During your engagement, you may discover opinions, habits, or values of your partner's that you hadn't seen before.

The fact is, whoever you marry will be very different from you. You can either accept who he is and learn how to live with your differences, or you can argue your point until you're blue in the face about the rightness or wrongness of black leather furniture. In short, you can choose to keep fighting about a problem that has no solution, or you can learn how to live with your differences.

Cynthia called me to talk after a month of Sundays spent at furniture stores because she had worked herself into a tizzy. "This is really scary," she told me. "If we can't decide what kind of couch we want, how will we make really important decisions, like where to live, what house to buy, or when to have a baby?" This line of thinking is what makes arguing during your engagement so frightening: every little fight gets magnified into full-scale panic.

"It's just a couch, for God's sake," she continued. "My parents would *never* spend four weekends arguing about what couch to buy."

Cynthia was right. Her parents, who had been married thirty years, wouldn't spend four consecutive Sundays searching and not finding a sofa. Why? Because after thirty years of marriage, they'd developed "their" style; they'd developed a design sense and aesthetic that pleased them both. What

Cynthia forgot is that her parents were also once engaged. They, too, had to learn how to join their lives (and design aesthetics) and unearth their differences. Thirty years earlier, her parents were beginners at marriage, just as Cynthia and Brian were now.

You and your fiancé are beginners at marriage, too. You've never been this intimately entwined with another person; you've never opened up your heart and your life this deeply to let another in. Even if you've been married before and know a bit about being married, you can't yet know how to be married to this specific person.

Adjusting to being engaged and to married life can be a lot like learning how to play tennis. When you first try to hit the ball across the net to your fiancé, your swing is off and balls fly everywhere—into the net, into the sky, and over the fence. But with practice—through months and years of sharing your day-to-day lives so intimately—the balls will stop flying in every direction, and you'll be able to volley, hitting back and forth, smoothly, confidently, and securely, because you'll know each other so well, at a depth you've never experienced before.

But you're not there yet, nor should you be, and that concept caused Cynthia to sigh with relief. "No wonder we can't find a couch we both like," said Cynthia. "We've never done this before." Then she came up with her own analogy about what they were going through as an engaged couple: "It's kind of like we're learning how to ride a tandem bike," she said. "We definitely still need our training wheels."

"By the way," she asked me, laughing, "they don't make black leather, shabby-chic sofas, do they?"

The Emotional To-Do List Item #9
Are You Still Being Polite?

 Now that you're engaged, you're journeying to a new level of intimacy and being more real than you were when you were just dating. You're seeing sides of each other that you never knew existed—flashes of anger, raw wounds, and humiliating insecurities. You're getting to know each other as real, vulnerable human beings, and you're learning how to be more deeply intimate with each other.

Or at least you should be. Are you still being polite? Are you still biting your tongue? Are you holding back your true self from your fiancé? Are you afraid to let down your guard and be your real, messy, human self? If so, why? What are you afraid of? What might happen if he sees all of you?

Now is not the time to play-act or pretend you're someone you're not. Showing your true colors one, two, or three years into your marriage and discovering you can't make it work will be painful and unfair to both of you. Now is the time to get to know each other—unvarnished, unscripted, unplugged.

Knockdowns and Drag-Outs

Nothing can seem scarier during your engagement than having a blowout with your fiancé. In the heat of the moment, you see new aspects of his personality that you wished didn't exist (and he sees yours, too), and you may say things you wish you could take back. Arguments like this can shake you to the core, causing you to reassess your relationship and wonder if you should go through with the wedding. But major arguments during your engagement can also bring the two of you much closer.

Five months before their wedding, Carrie and Alex were in real-estate hell: she was selling her apartment; he was moving into it until it was sold; and they were looking for a new nest of their own to buy. Oh, and they were planning their two-hundred-guest wedding. Carrie and Alex were under what's called "cluster stress," or the simultaneous occurrence of many life transitions and stressors. I think most engaged couples experience cluster stress since you're going through inner psychological transitions from single to married while at the same time planning your wedding, moving, and learning how to live together. It's a lot for two people to take on at once.

When Carrie and Alex fell in love with an apartment, they flew into high gear. They gathered their tax returns and financial information and headed to the broker's office to fill out a mortgage application.

Laying her financial life bare in front of Alex made Carrie feel more vulnerable than she had anticipated. She was worried he'd criticize her for not investing her 401(k) as efficiently as she should, or something like that. So she was relieved when the focus turned to Alex. "Do you owe any student loans?" asked the broker.

"About thirty thousand dollars," Alex replied.

"How about a car loan?"

"Are you kidding? I drive a 1991 Honda Civic!"

"Any credit-card debt?"

"About nine thousand dollars."

"What?" Carrie blurted out. She flew off the handle at Alex, right there in front of the mortgage broker. "I knew you had student loans, but now you're telling me you've been carrying around nine thousand dollars on your credit card?"

She was enraged both at his irresponsibility (she didn't believe in carrying balances on credit cards; how could she marry someone who did?) and at his withholding this information from her. "What else was he hiding?" she thought. For the next hour, as Alex and the broker combed through his financials, Carrie seethed.

In the parking lot, Carrie let him have it. "When were you planning to tell me about the nine thousand dollars?" she yelled. "Were you going to hide it from me forever? What about the apartment? Is your debt going to jeopardize our chances of getting it? Is it going to affect *my* credit score once we're married?"

They drove to her apartment in icy silence. "I can't be with you right now," Carrie barked at Alex. She went into the bedroom, slammed the door, and threw a tantrum. "I lost control," she told me. "I threw pillows across the room. I yelled. I was so mad at him for hiding the credit-card debt and for maybe endangering our chance to buy that apartment. And I was scared, too, about the person I was marrying: Was he really the responsible guy I thought he was? I questioned everything about him, and about us." Carrie eventually collapsed on her bed, curled into the fetal position, and sobbed. "That's when I heard a little knock at the door."

"Can I come in?" Alex asked.

After the fit she'd just thrown, Carrie's first reaction was "No!" She felt ashamed about getting so out of control.

Alex tiptoed in and curled up behind her on the bed. "I know you're mad," he whispered in her ear. "But I can't change the situation, and I can't make the nine-thousand-dollar debt disappear." He held her tight, told her he was sorry and that he loved her.

"His sweetness softened me," she said. "It was a turning point, when I realized that I still loved him even though I had been angrier at him than I had ever been at another human being. And he still loved me, even after the fit I threw." With rivers of mascara running down her cheeks, Carrie realized that she had never been that real, raw, or authentic with a man before. She'd never shown anybody that ugly side of herself. She'd never felt as vulnerable or, oddly, as loved by another person as she did in that moment. Carrie had let Alex see her at her most unkempt and out of control, and he not only tolerated it but loved her through it.

"I look back on that fight with a painful sort of fondness because it brought us so much closer," she said. "Before it, I thought of Alex as being Mr. Businessman, having every-thing in order and being a bit superior to me. But hearing about the credit-card debt, which he racked up just out of college, I realized he wasn't perfect. He came off his pedestal and became real to me, just a guy living his life.

"I learned that our relationship really was a safe place for me to be me," she continued. "I'd never had that with a man before, and I felt really lucky to be spending my life with Alex." That day, Carrie saw what her marriage-to-be could handle, and it could handle a lot.

Talking About the Nitty-Gritty
One Bride's Experience

Early on in our relationship and throughout our engagement, my fiancé and I talked about the tough things. Children (he wanted three, I wanted one; we settled on two). What we wanted to do for holidays. How often we talk to our families. What's okay to share about our relationship with friends and family, and what's not. We really got down to the nitty-gritty, and stayed there, because we were both aware that we were laying the foundation of our marriage.

—*Renee, married eight months*

The Wavering of That Lovin' Feeling

Engaged women call me all the time worrying that they've become their own worst nightmares: nitpicky nags who are hypercritical of their husbands-to-be. Sarah, who struggled with the end of her identity as Sarah the Sociologist, became preoccupied with her fiancé's bald spot. "Before we were engaged, I thought it was cute," she told me. "Now I can't take my eyes off it. I keep thinking, 'Did he lose more hair today? Will our sons be bald? How can I buy him Rogaine without offending him?'"

"Is his baldness a reason not to marry him?" I asked. "Do you think maybe you're fixating on his bald spot as a way of ignoring more serious problems with your fiancé or with your relationship?"

"Oh my God, no!" she said. "Not at all!"

In my experience, when brides-to-be know that they want to walk down the aisle yet cannot stop themselves from nit-picking, there are usually three possible explanations.

One is that little obsessions like this can be a way for you to come to terms with who the man you're marrying really is. It helps the reality sink in. When she was a little girl, Sarah never envisioned her knight in shining armor as a bald guy, yet here she was, marrying one. Spotlighting it like this was helping her change the image in her mind to match her reality.

A second explanation is that being hypercritical of your fiancé in your mind (or to his face) diverts your attention and energy away from the ending of your life as a single woman and daughter that you're facing. It's easier sometimes to nag him — because he always runs late, is a bit of a slob, watches too much TV, or is bald — than it is to feel and process your sadness.

That made sense to Sarah. "I get it," she said. "Whenever I get sick of dealing with the ending of my identity as only a sociologist, I unconsciously switch gears and focus on his bald spot. His bald spot is like a little vacation from my grief."

"The key," I told Sarah, "is to catch yourself being hyper-critical of him."

When you find yourself focusing on your fiancé's bald spot, excessive golfing, credit-card debt, or whatever [insert your fiancé's characteristic that you obsess about here], ask yourself this quesion: What in my grief work am I avoiding?

When you're devoting so much time, emotion, energy, and thought to letting go of your single life and family, there's not much left for your fiancé. Emotionally, you may be running on empty, so it's challenging to feel sexy and lusty, warm and fuzzy, causing your love for your fiancé to go underground. "A lot of time, I feel like my love for Jake's behind a screen," Sarah said. When I ask brides-to-be about their sex lives, almost across the board their response is, "What sex life?" During your engagement, most of your emotional energy — including your libido — is focused on your past. Being in the present with your fiancé can seem nearly impossible.

Finally, a third possibility is that you're just plain mad at your fiancé and are focusing on his faults so you can stay angry. What are you angry at? It may sound crazy, but brides-to-be blame their fiancés for causing this chaos in their emotional lives. "If we weren't getting married," the thinking goes, "I wouldn't be feeling all this loss." That's true: if you didn't love each other so much that you wanted to get married, you wouldn't have to go through all these changes. And yet, you want to get married, so you're stuck in a conundrum, and you blame him for it.

You may also be irrationally blaming your fiancé because you'll never have those first days and weeks of your relationship back. You'll never fall in love with him for the first time again. You'll probably never spend entire weekends in bed together or dance cheek-to-cheek for hours on end as you did during those first months together. In fact, MRI scans of the brain show that there are different places in the brain for new love and for long-term commitment. As you're moving toward 'til death do you part, the activity in your brain has changed location as well; the new-love place is still active, but to a significantly lesser degree. I often hear brides-to-be complain that the thrilling new blush of love has passed, never to be had again — and it's perfectly normal and natural to be bummed out about it.

Even though the wild intoxication of your new love has mellowed, a deeper, long-lasting bond is growing between you. That's the best news, since that's the direction you and your fiancé are headed. You'll get glimpses of the deepening of your relationship throughout your engagement — be on the lookout for them. Even the couples who went head-to-head in this chapter did so. Cynthia and Brian eventually found a couch — a nonpuffy, streamlined design with a faint white-on-white floral print. More significant than buying a piece of furniture, however, was what they learned about being together in a long-term, committed relationship with each other. "We still fight, and it's still challenging sometimes to live together," Cynthia told me. "But now when we're at cross-purposes, one of us stops and says, 'Is this a black leather, shabby-chic sofa?' It's become shorthand for us, a way to acknowledge our differences in a lighthearted, fun, silly way. It's code for 'Let's take a step back,' and it always makes us laugh."

Even Carrie and Alex, who had the blowup over his nine-thousand-dollar credit-card balance, dropped into a deeper level of partnership through their time together in real-estate hell. When it came time to sell Carrie's apartment, Alex took responsibility for some tasks, much to Carrie's surprise and delight. (After so many years on her own, she assumed all jobs would fall to her.) He'd deal with the lawyers and real-estate agents, leaving Carrie to focus on her strengths, which involved marketing and showing the apartment to prospective buyers. Selling the property by themselves was still stressful, but as buyer after buyer toured it, Carrie and Alex developed a wordless communication. They could tell by each other's looks and body language what to do and say next, and that bonded them even more deeply.

"Through the entire process of selling my apartment, for the first time in my life, I felt really partnered," Carrie told me. "I didn't have to do everything myself; Alex had my back when I needed help. We were a team."

When the apartment sold for sixteen thousand dollars over their asking price, Alex was downright impressed with his girl. "You're a natural saleswoman! I'm so proud of you!" Alex said to her as they did a little swing dance around the living room. Living through this experience together had brought out the best—and the worst—in both Carrie and Alex, and through it all they became even more real, more loving, and more deeply bonded.

Cold Feet Alert: Temporary vs. Permanent Problems

 When a bride-to-be can't take the plunge and slide her wedding invitations into the mailbox, it's a sign that she needs to slow down and pay attention to her anxiety. She needs to articulate and express her fears and concerns and evaluate them one by one. Here's how.

Karen was prompted to attend my "Cold Feet: Red Flags or Just Jitters?" workshop when she couldn't pack up to move into her fiancé's apartment three months before their wedding.

"I can't make myself pack boxes," she said. "I sit on the floor and stare at them and cry. The only time I feel okay is when I let myself think of staying put. I think that means I should call off the wedding."

Not so fast, Karen. First we had to look at what was bothering her.

"This shouldn't be a big deal, but I'm a Democrat, and he's a Republican," she said. "But it's so dumb to be worried about that. Our political discussions get heated sometimes, but that shouldn't stop us from getting married."

Karen was trying to talk herself out of her feelings. I stopped her, interjecting, "Okay, what else?"

"What else?"

Thinking for a moment, she said, "This is stupid, too, but I'm a vegetarian, and he's not."

"What else?"

"Well, he's a real neat freak, and I'm . . . well, as my mother says, I'm 'not so interested in cleaning.'"

"What else?"

"Here's the big one," she sighs. "My fiancé suffered a head injury playing football in high school, and he has some memory loss. He has to stick to strict routines and keep detailed lists just to accomplish everyday things that the rest of us do automatically. I'm really wondering if I want to live with all the limits and lists and procedures for the rest of my life."

"What else?"

"This seems so lightweight in comparison, but I've had a really hard time planning the wedding. Details are totally not my thing, and I actually kind of hate it. But with Jamie's memory problems, the wedding planning has fallen almost entirely on my shoulders. Being responsible for this huge event is stressing me out."

Karen downloaded her thoughts like this for half an hour. Talking freely and openly about her worries—getting them off her chest without analyzing them or judging herself—helped relieve her burden. Her body language relaxed; her jaw loosened, and her brow softened. She even laughed at herself toward the end. "I'm digging deep here," she said, "but the way he leaves his cereal bowl in the sink instead of putting it into the dishwasher before he leaves for work makes me crazy."

As Karen's worries spilled out, I jotted down some brief notes. When I handed the long list to her, she inhaled sharply, her anxiety spiking again. Seeing her worries—from the minute to the major—in one place was overwhelming. But before she could get too wound up, I passed her a piece of paper with two categories: ISSUES THAT ARE TEMPORARY and ISSUES THAT ARE PERMANENT. Her task: to assign each concern to one category.

It didn't take Karen long to create a new list, and when she reviewed it, she was surprised that she felt really happy. First off, by categorizing "wedding-planning stress" as temporary, Karen saw that that major stress would be gone after the wedding. Same for her sudden fears about moving into Jamie's apartment. Deep down, she knew in her heart she wanted to live with him. The grip of fear she was experiencing over it was, she recognized, passing and normal. She'd never been a big fan of change. In time— a few months, she figured—she'd become accustomed to it, which is why that issue fell into the temporary category as well.

Karen placed their differences in diet under the permanent category and acknowledged that it wasn't a huge deal. As long as he cooked his own pork butt, she and her legumes weren't affected one bit. The Republican thing also belonged in the permanent category; his views weren't budging. But they had fun talking politics, and they'd learned how to agree to disagree; marriage wouldn't take that ability away.

Jamie's memory loss was a permanent fact of life for them as a married couple, and Karen's response surprised her. "When I see Jamie's memory loss on the permanent list, what I really see is what's missing, and that's how much I love him," she said. "His memory loss is going to affect every single day of my life. But what he suffered and what he overcame is what's made him the kind, warm, patient, compassionate, empathetic, loving man he is today. I don't know who Jamie would be without the football accident. Although it's going to be a challenge at times, it's also what makes him so lovable.

"The other thing that's missing from this list," Karen laughed, "is how great our sex life is!"

After Karen categorized her fears, she felt at peace. She could dismiss her wedding stress, knowing it would soon pass. She saw that she'd blown her fears about vegetarianism and politics way out of proportion. And she realized that her greatest fear about the legacy of Jamie's accident was in fact an essential aspect of what she loved about him.

The cold feet Karen felt as she packed up her apartment turned out to be a blessing in disguise. By working through her worries, she left no stone unturned, no question unexamined. The end result: she was entering her marriage with her eyes wide open to its challenges, but also with a clear connection to the reasons why she was choosing Jamie as her husband. Six weeks later, Karen stood confidently and happily beside Jamie at the altar.

This exercise of articulating fears and worries one by one was useful for Terri, too, but in a different way: it helped her clearly see that she did in fact need to call off her wedding.

Before doing the exercise, Terri had been a master at talking herself out of her fears. But seeing all her fears on one page, she saw that she'd been living in a state of denial about her fiancé.

The majority of Terri's fears fell under the permanent heading, including their differences in politics and religious beliefs. Terri also saw several red flags: her fiancé's anger, which scared her at times; his drinking and marijuana use; his emotional neediness; how he withdrew when she was stressed (when she needed him to support and hold her); her lack of respect for the way he handled money; her gnawing sense that "I could do better."

Seeing her worries listed together like this, the reality of who her fiancé was and what a future with him would be like became undeniable. For her health, safety, and happiness, Terri decided to call off the wedding and pull the plug on their relationship before it fell under the permanent category, too.

CHAPTER 6

The Girls

Keeping Your Single Girlfriends Close

Friendship Fiascoes

Many brides-to-be imagine that their engagements will be filled with frilly, feminine times with their best single girlfriends. They have visions of giggling in the bridal-shop dressing room as their best friend tries on hideous maid-of-honor dresses and flipping through bridal magazines together as their toes soak in pedicure tubs.

You may very well have some uncomplicated fun like that, especially with your married girlfriends. In fact, during your engagement you may find yourself turning to your married pals more than ever for their wisdom, guidance, and support. (They understand how stressful and infuriating it can be to talk on the phone with an out-of-control mother-in-law-to-be.) Things between you and your single girlfriends, however, can often be much more complicated, as Leann discovered one day over lunch.

Leann and her two best girlfriends called themselves "The Gang of Three." For five years, they'd been through the ups and downs of single life in the big city together. "We're like Carrie Bradshaw and her friends, but we have a lot less sex than they do," she told a workshop of brides-to-be, laughing.

In their careers, they were one another's biggest cheer-leaders and supporters. At bars, they acted as "wing women," helping one another scope out cute guys or ward off undesirable ones. During boyfriendless stretches, they were vacation partners and movie buddies. When a breakup occurred, they jumped into high gear: one would bring the Kleenex, the other would bring the wine and the Ben & Jerry's. The Gang of Three was tight.

When Leann started dating Rick, she naturally spent less time with her girlfriends, as each member of the Gang did when a new boyfriend entered the picture; everyone understood that Rick had become her movie buddy and vacation partner. However, while the tightness of the Gang of Three had always varied as boyfriends came and went, when Leann and Rick got *engaged*, something changed.

One day, about two months into her engagement, Leann was sitting at brunch with the Gang and started talking about the stress she was feeling about the wedding—how they couldn't decide on a location, how much everything was costing, how being engaged wasn't the happiest time of her life. She'd been dealing with all the wedding problems on her own for the last two weeks, and she'd been looking forward to seeing her friends to vent and ask their advice. She was about halfway through her saga when one of her friends interrupted her.

"You know what?" she said. "I don't want to hear about your so-called problems."

"What?" Leann asked, shocked. Ouch. That verbal slap in the face hurt Leann, and she was stunned by her friend's blunt comment. It had never occurred to Leann that her best friends wouldn't want to hear what was happening during this pivotal time in her life. She'd been so consumed by the wedding and the changes in her life—leaving her single life, her family, and her lighthearted dating days—that she hadn't considered *their* reactions for a minute.

"I felt chastised by her, and I got her message, loud and clear," Leann said. "She didn't want to hear about my wedding, so I wasn't going to tell her." Leann left lunch indignant, offended, and more than a little hurt. "I never expected that during my engagement, I'd feel so distant from my best friends," she said. Leann felt isolated and alone, cut off from her closest girlfriends, with whom—until that lunch, at least—she had shared her deepest fears, feelings, and insecurities about every aspect of her life.

Leann's experience is not uncommon. In my workshops, brides-to-be often talk about the chill that descended upon warm friendships after they got engaged. One woman talked of being disappointed that her single friends didn't share her excitement about her wedding: "Whenever I start talking about my wedding, they get blank stares on their faces, like they're waiting for me to shut up about it all." Another described how she was sharing less of herself with her single friends now that she was engaged: "I'm afraid that talking about how happy I am will hurt their feelings because they don't have boyfriends right now. So I don't tell them, and not saying anything about the biggest thing in my life feels weird because before I got engaged, I told them everything!" A third bride-to-be felt let down by her best friend: "I can't get my maid of honor to focus on anything, and she's really pissing me off! I'm thinking of telling her I've changed my mind." Another bride-to-be lamented how her interests had changed since getting engaged: "I don't want to go out to bars with my girlfriends on Friday nights the way I used to, and my fiancé and I don't have any couple friends yet. My engagement's turning out to be kind of lonely." A final bride-to-be decided to take the path of least resistance: "Dealing with my single friends is too complicated these days. I'm finding it's easier to spend time with the new friends I've made in the Knot chat room. They totally understand what I'm going through."

Sometimes, simply eradicating a problem can seem like the most expeditious route. Disinvite a belligerent bridesmaid to be in your wedding party, and you've got one less thing to stress about on your wedding day. Stop going out to bars with your single girlfriends on Friday nights, and none of you has to deal directly with the differences between being engaged and being single. Forge new relationships with your online, about-to-be married pals, and you can march forward into your new, married life unencumbered by the emotional baggage of old friends.

Many engaged women choose the easy route during their engagements and jettison their single friends. In the long run, however, it's the brides-to-be who suffer. Having burned too many bridges with their close friends before the wedding, they wake up one day in a new marriage without any of the old supports, joys, pleasures, and familiarities that come with these female friendships. Brides-to-be who opt for the short-term relief of not dealing with their single friends during their engagements end up losing out.

Your Girls, Yourself

For most women, their close friends are an essential part of who they are. Unlike family, which often need you to perform a certain role and behave a certain way, your friends love you for who you genuinely are. Some people consider friends their "chosen family"; this is an interesting take on these important people in your life. Think about it: of all the billions of people in the world, you and your friends have sought one another out to be confidantes and intimates.

You have likely grown close with your friends over time and through shared experiences. You've watched one another pursue dreams, reach heights, fall flat on your faces, and try again. You've witnessed flings, crushes, hookups, and affairs, and you've seen one another fall in (and out of) love. You've supported one another, challenged one another, fought with one another, and loved one another through it all. You've probably known your best girlfriends far longer than you've known your fiancé. And in some ways, they know you better than he does.

So it's no big surprise that when you announced your engagement, your closest single girlfriends felt a bit displaced and replaced by him, causing a mixed-up mess of emotions. They feel happy for you that you've found your man and are having the wedding of your dreams. But they may also feel sad for themselves about losing some degree of intimacy with you, and maybe they're a little scared, too; you found your Mr. Right, and your wedding makes them wonder if they'll find their guy. They also may feel angry that you're going off into the sunset and leaving them behind. In short, your single friends are probably having many mixed emotions about your marriage.

Brides-to-be and their closest friends rarely share their feelings about how the marriage might affect their friendships. Some engaged women are in denial that anything will change in their friendships with women; they believe (or want to believe) that they will continue the same frequency of talking on the phone, going out, and sharing intimacies. Others don't think they'll be missed all that much. And some brides-to-be feel guilty, like they're abandoning their friends, and they're afraid to bring up the topic.

For their part, the girlfriends often don't feel *entitled* to having any negative emotional reaction to their friends' marriages; they think they should just be happy for their friend, and let her go off quietly into married life. They think they need to put up, shut up, and be okay with losing one more friend to the black hole that married people seem to disappear into.

Talking It Out

If brides-to-be and their closest friends don't talk openly and honestly about the changes in their friendships, the emotions will still come out—and often out of nowhere. This is exactly what happened to Megan and her best friend (and maid of honor), Brittany.

Shortly after Megan and Dirk got engaged, Brittany invited the happy couple out for Sunday brunch to celebrate their engagement and to thank Megan for asking her to play such a big part in her wedding. When the mimosas arrived, Brittany toasted the couple's future. "I'm so happy for you guys, and your wedding is going to be amazing," she said. "But I'm going to have to get very, very drunk to enjoy it."

"What?" Megan asked.

"I don't have a boyfriend, and everybody else is coming as a couple, so I'm going to have to get drunk to get through it," Brittany responded, matter-of-factly.

Brittany's comment pissed Megan right off. "Our wedding's in six months, and she *already* thinks that she's going to have to get wasted in order to get through it?" Megan later commented to other brides-to-be in a workshop. Megan fumed silently through brunch, questioning her desire to have Brittany in her wedding party. In addition, she felt embarrassed in front of Dirk—ashamed that her best friend would say such a thing. It was completely out of character for Brittany, and Megan was afraid that Dirk would get the wrong impression of her. It was important to her that her husband and her best friend get along, and she worried that things weren't starting off on the right foot.

A few days later, Megan's anger at Brittany softened because she had a sense of where her best friend might be coming from, even if her delivery of the message lacked tact. "Before meeting Dirk, I went to a zillion weddings as a single woman, and I know how awkward and awful it can be," she told the workshop. "You're seated at the reception next to the bride's loser cousin. You have to wait for your friends' husbands to ask you to dance (whoopee!). And you go back to your expensive hotel room alone while your friend is in the honeymoon suite, and you stay up all night worrying about whether or not you'll meet Mr. Right. I don't know if Brittany's thinking about all this, but it's possible that that's what the 'I have to get drunk' comment was about."

"Is it possible that you are worrying about the status of your friendship as well?" I asked Megan.

"God, I hadn't even thought about that," she replied. "But it's true. I don't know every single tiny detail in her life the way I used to because I've been spending all my time with Dirk for the last eighteen months. I don't feel as connected and close to her, and that definitely makes me sad, too."

As Megan spoke, all the other brides-to-be in the workshop nodded their heads in agreement. Engaged women, it turns out, often feel the same loss of intimacy as their friends do. Sadness over the changes happens on both sides of the friendship equation.

It's up to you to ameliorate the situation, I told the brides-to-be. (Your girlfriends will assume you're happy, happy,

happy!) Open the conversation by telling your friend that, plain and simple, you miss her (assuming you do). Acknowledge that your upcoming marriage will impact your friendship with her, but reiterate how important she is to you, how much you love her, and how much you value her as a friend. And then ask her what your engagement has been like for her and what thoughts and feelings she may have about it.

Sound scary? It can be. Megan didn't want to have this conversation with Brittany, but she knew that for the sake of their friendship, she needed to. Megan walked out of the workshop on a mission to repair her friendship with Brittany. A few months later, she let me know what transpired between them.

"After the workshop, I thought long and hard about how to approach Brittany about her 'gotta get drunk' comment," she told me. "I didn't want to come off as angry, and I didn't want to sound condescending or patronizing, as in, 'I'm so lucky to be getting married, and poor you, you're not getting married and you must feel bad about it.' It was a delicate line that I had to walk, and I had difficulty finding the right words."

She decided to speak from her heart. One afternoon, Megan invited Brittany to go on a hike, just the two of them. On the way up the mountain, they chitchatted about the wedding and work—nothing very real, meaningful, or personal, which was completely out of character for these two close friends, who'd always shared every detail in the past. Their conversation skimmed the surface the entire way up the trail. Megan was initially disappointed by their lack of connection, but it turned out to be a blessing in disguise: it provided the perfect opening for Megan.

"I gotta tell you, Brit, this is weird, what we're doing right now," Megan said, as she sat on a rock on top of the mountain, admiring the view below.

"What do you mean?" Brittany replied.

"We're being really polite with each other, dancing around each other, when what I really want to talk about is what's going on with us," Megan said. "I have all this huge stuff going on in my life that I want to talk to you about, but I'm afraid to bring it up after your comment at brunch about needing to get drunk at our wedding. It was a strange thing for you to say, and I've been thinking about it a lot."

"Me too," said Brittany. "I've been feeling really bad about that. I'm sorry."

"Thanks, but I'm really not looking for an apology," Megan clarified. "What matters is that we're talking about it. I don't know what's really going on in your life, and I know that I haven't been telling you as much about my life as I usually do. I guess what I'm saying is, I miss you."

What Megan said was enough to break down the wall that had been building between them since the brunch. Instead of getting angry at Brittany or feeling sorry for her, Megan focused on her own feelings of loss about their friendship, and on her feelings of responsibility for causing the change in the dynamic of their friendship because she was spending all her time with Dirk.

"It makes sense that you're with him all the time," Brittany said. "You're getting married to him soon, for God's sake. It's just a big change in my life, too, you know? It never really occurred to me before that your getting married was going to make me feel so, well, lonely. I feel like I've lost you a bit."

"I know, I know," said Megan. "I feel like I've lost you, too. This is so weird! And hard. Sometimes, I get mad at Dirk for taking me away from you, from us, from my old life. It's a lot more complicated than I thought it would be."

"But it feels better already, talking about it," Brittany said, quietly.

It certainly did, Megan told me. The doors to their friendship swung open again, and on top of that mountain, they talked openly with each other—about the changes in their friendships, about their struggles in life, about their fears. It felt like old times. It felt great.

Connected once again, the two friends bounded, frolicked, and played the whole way down the mountain. They reminisced, laughed, and poked fun at each other. Before they got into the car to head home, Megan stopped Brittany and gave her a big hug. "I know this is weird and hard for both of us, Brit," she said. "But you are my best friend, and it's important that you know how much I love you. I know things are going to change when I marry Dirk. They already have. But I can't and I won't do married life without you. Are you with me?"

Brittany was with her, and she showed her how much throughout Megan's wedding weekend. Not only did she look gorgeous in her pale pink bridesmaid's dress, she put herself second and supported Megan through everything. She gave the most touching and heartfelt speech at the rehearsal dinner, and she snuck a bottle of champagne past the wedding coordinator, to toast with Megan before she walked down the aisle. Megan knew her wedding weekend must have been hard and painful for Brittany, but Brittany didn't let it show. "I think she was able to be so emotionally present for me because she knew how important, cared for, and considered she was during my engagement," Megan said. "Brittany now knows how invested I am in continuing our friendship on an intimate, confidante level for the rest of our lives."

The Emotional To-Do List Item #10
Owning Your Behavior and Emotions

 Now that your relationship with your fiancé is number one in your life, you're likely giving less time, energy, and intimacy to your close girlfriends. This is normal, natural, and necessary. Still, the changing nature of your friendships as a result of your marriage-to-be impacts not only your friends, but you as well.

How have your behavior (frequency of phone calls, dinners with just the two of you, nights out with the girls) and your emotional investment (what you share, what you don't) in your friendships with your girlfriends changed since you started dating your fiancé? Since you got engaged?

Why do you think your behavior has changed? Sure, you've got a lot on your plate with the wedding, but what's at the core in your change of behavior? Do you see your girlfriends less because it heightens your sense of loss, because it makes you miss them more? Are you afraid of their reactions to your marriage-to-be, what they might be thinking and feeling? Are you feeling guilty for leaving them, so to speak? Explore what's really going on inside you.

Four Friends, Four Outcomes

When it was her turn to get married, Pauline made a point of being sensitive to her single girlfriends' feelings. Over the years, she had watched her group of single friends dwindle from a huge gang to a small handful. As one after another walked off into married life, Pauline's heart broke a little each time, as she prepared for the lessening of connection in their friendship. "Whenever somebody in our group got engaged and married, I was terribly excited for them," Pauline said. "But at the same time, I always thought to myself, 'What about me?' Not only did I feel like yet another friend was leaving me as she walked down the aisle, I also felt like the perpetual single girl. It made me wonder and worry a little about whether I'd get married someday, too."

When Pauline got engaged, she brought this keen awareness of the conflicting emotions that engagements and weddings had always evoked in her into her friendships. She wanted to treat her friends with a sensitivity and awareness that she herself hadn't always received. She refused to alienate them by talking ad nauseum about the wedding, for instance, or to dump them for her fiancé—things she had experienced previously with other friends. Her goal: for her precious friendships with her single friends to survive her engagement intact. Her plan: to be honest and real about the effects of her engagement on herself, on her friends, and on their friendships. The result: four different friendships with four different outcomes.

Friend #1: Because of past broken hearts, Pauline's roommate Gina had avoided relationships for many years, yet deep down she still longed to be married. So for Gina, watching Pauline fall in love and get engaged was bittersweet.

Lucky for Pauline, Gina was the type of person who put her feelings on the table. "I'm so happy for you, Pauline," Gina volunteered just days after Pauline got engaged. "And I hope it's okay to tell you this, but watching you find Mr. Right just makes me worry about myself, you know?"

With Gina, Pauline had it easy because Gina was able to separate her own feelings into two categories: sad for herself and happy for Pauline. Gina didn't shy away from her feelings of sadness; she didn't push the sadness away because it was real for her. And voicing her sadness—expressing and sharing it with Pauline—was essential because it made their interactions real and honest. Both Gina and Pauline knew where the other stood, how the other felt, and how the other valued the friendship.

"Gina turned out to be a wonderful support and a voice of reason during my engagement," Pauline says, in gratitude and amazement. "She could step outside of what she was feeling personally to walk with me through some of the tough emotional stuff. Gina became a big cheerleader for me, encouraging me in my happiness. It was so gracious of her."

Friend #2: Pauline's other roommate, Samantha, couldn't contain her sadness over Pauline's moving out of the house they shared, and constantly expressed it, albeit indirectly or passive-aggressively. Whenever Pauline brought home her veil or boxes of dried rose petals, for example, Samantha's reaction was a muted, "Yeah, that's nice."

"It seemed like every little wedding-related thing represented my leaving her," said Pauline. "She never expressed it outright, but I could see it in her eyes. I wanted to bring it up, but I was too scared to talk about it with her so directly."

Pauline decided that the best thing for their friendship was for her to back off. Once again, she was allowing her friend to express whatever emotions she was experiencing. She let Samantha go and crossed her fingers that once life settled down after the wedding, Samantha would reengage in the friendship. And that's precisely what happened. Samantha was cool to Pauline on her wedding day and for the first six months of her marriage, but in time, Samantha started reaching out and making plans. It was like old times again. Samantha just needed her space, and Pauline let her have it.

Friend #3: Three months before the wedding, Pauline took Stephanie out for coffee. "I told her how I had always felt when friends got married—happy for them, sad and scared for me," Pauline recounted. "I even ventured to say, 'Maybe you're feeling some of the same things?'"

"No, no, no, I'm fine," said Stephanie, glossing over what for Pauline had been a painful part of friends' weddings. Stephanie didn't — or couldn't — acknowledge that she was having any of those complex feelings.

"Really?" Pauline asked. "At my friend Christie's wedding last year, I was a wreck on her wedding day. I felt really scared about my own future."

"I didn't feel anything like that," Stephanie said, close-lipped and defensively. The conversation went nowhere.

As the wedding approached, a wall went up between the two friends, and they slowly drifted apart. The precise thing that Pauline had wanted to avoid after the wedding came to pass: when they saw each other at church, there were big hugs and lots of checking in, but no real personal involvement or intimacy. They just continued to drift apart. It's possible that Pauline approached this conversation with Stephanie from the wrong direction: she tried to get Stephanie to talk about *herself*, to admit to having some difficult, embarrassing, unorthodox feelings about Pauline's wedding. Stephanie may have felt pushed or under pressure to bare her soul, and nobody reacts well to that type of interrogation. If Pauline had begun the conversation by talking more about her own experience — her sadness about the changes in her friendships, her anxieties about the future, her feelings of loss — there's a good chance that Stephanie may have felt more at ease about sharing where she was and how she was feeling.

Friend #4: Amy felt plain old hurt when Pauline got engaged. "She tried hard to be happy for me," she remembers. "She gave me a big hug and ogled my ring, but the look in her eyes said something very different. I have a feeling my engagement reminded Amy not only that she wasn't where she wanted to be in life, but also how far away she was from achieving it." Pauline understood that look in Amy's eyes; it was a feeling she knew well from her own experience.

Amy's reaction to Pauline's engagement—her powerful hurt, her longing for a romantic relationship, and her palpable fear about her own future—was the rawest of the group. In contrast to her conversation with Stephanie, this time Pauline didn't push for her friend to bare her feelings. Instead, she bared her own, revealing her sadness about the inevitable changes in her friendships and her fear of losing Amy. Pauline's openness made it safe for Amy to join in that intimate space. As a result, Pauline and Amy were able to "go there"—to discuss and explore the feelings both women had about Pauline's marriage, its effect on their friendship, and, most significantly, the uncomfortable feelings it had stirred in each of them. Pauline's ability to show her vulnerability allowed Amy to share hers, and this saved—even deepened—their friendship. "Of my friends, Amy and I remained closest after I got married," said Pauline.

Bridesmaids Speak Out

I've been a bridesmaid six times, and I'll never forget how one particular friend made a huge effort to show me how much she valued our friendship. In the middle of her wedding craziness, she flew across the country—taking time off work and away from her fiancé—to see me and enjoy our friendship. We talked about her wedding, of course, but we also talked about the real stuff of our lives and our friendship. It meant a lot to me.

—*Jeri*

I ended up feeling used by one bride-friend. I think she picked me to be her only attendant because she thinks I'm "well-bred" and I'd know how to do all the showers, luncheons, and parties. But it was a huge responsibility and expense for one person to pull off. We never talked about *us*—our friendship or what it meant for me to be her maid of honor; it was all about the external stuff. My feeling after her wedding? I'm broke and resentful, and I don't know how close I want to be with this friend anymore.

—*Victoria*

Most brides just talk about their weddings, but one friend of mine talked about herself—how scared she was to make a lifelong commitment, how weird it was not to be single anymore. We met for drinks a lot, and she was real with me every time. I really felt included, in an intimate way, as she prepared to become a wife, and it was cool. An honor, even, to be let in that close.

—*Helene*

Cold Feet Alert: Calling Off Your Wedding—A Practical Guide

This is the final Cold Feet Alert in this book.

If, after putting your relationship and your feelings about your fiancé on the couch in the five preceding Cold Feet Alerts, you've decided that you do in fact to need to call off your wedding, here's an idea of what you might expect.

Calling off your wedding will be one of the most difficult things you will ever do in your life, but remember: if you do not want to commit yourself to your fiancé for a lifetime, you must call it off.

The high drama of telling your fiancé, family, and friends will last a week or so. You'll shock everyone's system, and it will probably be an emotional time for everyone involved. Let everyone have their feelings, and weather the storm. After a week or so, everyone will begin to adjust to the reality that you're not getting married and eventually move back into their own lives. In time, the drama will end.

Your fiancé may feel devastated, enraged, betrayed, humiliated, ashamed, embarrassed, afraid, furious about the money spent, and a thousand other high-intensity emotions. But in a few days, weeks, or months, he will be okay. He'll get over it. He'll heal, and he'll move on.

Your family may be shocked, especially if you've hidden your ambivalent feelings from them, as most brides-to-be do. They might be angry at the outlay of money for the wedding itself, but ultimately, they'll be relieved that you made the best decision for yourself. Your long-term happiness is worth a $20,000 (or $200,000) reception. Really, it is.

His family may be angry; they'll think you've hurt and humiliated their son. There's not much you can do about that; all you can hope is that one day they'll realize that you made the best decision for you and for him. Their son deserves to be married to someone who wants to be married to him, and if that's not you, he—and they—will be grateful, eventually.

Your friends will support you. They'll be fine with swallowing the cost of $400 plane tickets and $150 hotel rooms because they want you to be happy. They'll probably want to make plans to be with you on what was to be your wedding weekend. Let them.

Your guests will understand. A few days after you've spoken with your fiancé, your family, his family, and your close friends, contact each guest personally by phone, letter, or e-mail, and inform them that the wedding has been called off, that you're sorry for the inconvenience, and that you appreciate their support—of you and your fiancé—during this difficult time.

Then there's you. You may feel a combination of huge relief, horrible guilt, regret, and uncertainty. You'll also probably feel like the bad guy. It will likely be a tough, tough time. Or it could go really smoothly—you'll never know until you do it. It's important to get emotional support from family and friends at a time like this. You may also want to consider counseling so that you can unearth the reasons why you almost walked down the aisle with the wrong person, so that you don't make the same mistake again.

A reassuring resource for women who've called off their weddings is a book titled *There Goes the Bride*, by Rachel Safier. In it you'll read detailed stories of sixty-two "Almost Brides"—women who called off their own weddings or who had their weddings called off. This book addresses the emotional and practical aspects of calling off a wedding. How-to's include what to do about the ring, how to get money back from vendors, telling the officiant, informing the newspapers, sending back gifts, selling bridesmaids' dresses on eBay, and more.

In the short term, calling off your wedding may be difficult and sometimes awful. The guilt, the money spent, the loss of relationship with your fiancé, the fear that there's no one else out there—

all this may at times overwhelm you. But something deep within you knows that you're making the right decision, and you must trust that.

Here's some perspective: in one to two years' time, you'll look back on the week you called off your wedding, and your memory of it will be hazy. You'll feel clear and certain that you made the right decision. You'll have grown immensely from this challenge, you'll probably be in a new relationship, and you'll have learned so much about yourself.

The short term can be tough, but calling off a wedding now, before it happens, is better than the pain of a divorce.

Stage Two

BRIDGING

CHAPTER 7

Crossing the Bridge
Your New Life Takes Shape

Looking Forward, Not Back

When Sarah (the Sociologist) looked out her window ten weeks before her wedding and saw the UPS guy approaching her front door with two big boxes containing her wedding invitations, she felt something she hadn't in months: excited. "I threw open door so fast that I startled the deliveryman," she told me. "Adrenaline raced through my body. My heart was beating fast. Seeing the boxes of invitations made the wedding seem very real to me—it suddenly hit me that it was all really happening!"

Sarah tried to wait until her fiancé got home from work to open the boxes, but she couldn't hold back. She got a pair of scissors and sliced through the packing tape. "They were just beautiful," she said. "So much more beautiful with our names on them, instead of the generic 'Mr. and Mrs. Smith' from the big invitation books. I ran my fingers over the raised lettering of my name and Jake's name, and I was filled with peace and love. In that moment, I felt more ready to be married than I had ever felt before."

After a couple of minutes, Sarah tore herself away from the invitations and reply cards and forced herself to get back to her work. It was the end of the semester, and the professor had papers to grade. Her thoughts, however, kept circling back to the invitations—how happy they made her feel and how new that feeling of happiness was. "I'd been anxious for most of our engagement," she said, "focusing only on how getting married was going to hurt my career, how it might thwart my ambition and change the professional identity I'd worked so hard to create. But when the invitations arrived, the jolt of joy I felt was so strong and new that it seemed to shock me out of my sadness and anxiety. I was on a high for the rest of the day."

Throughout the afternoon, whenever Sarah finished grading a paper, she rewarded herself by visiting the invitations that were sitting on her dining-room table. As she fingered the heavy card stock, she realized that her attitude about getting married had actually been shifting, slowly and subtly, for the last few weeks. Her reaction to the invitations was the strongest sign yet, but there'd been other signals, too.

A month earlier, Sarah and Jake had taken a long weekend away at the beach, just the two of them. It was hot, and they drove with the windows down and the radio cranked up. At the beach, they bodysurfed and made huge sand castles together. It was a weekend of play and fun.

"Before Jake, I would have had classical music playing in the car, and I would have taken long, quiet walks on the beach,"

Sarah told me. "With him, I'm much more 'in' the world; I feel much more alive. In the two years that we've been dating, Jake's exposed me to rock and jazz and R&B, which I didn't know anything about before him—and I'm loving it. I've learned how to play more; life's more fun with him. And that weekend at the beach really drove all these positive changes home for me. I saw, more clearly than I had in months, how having him in my life enhances and enriches my every day.

"I'm also finally seeing that being married isn't going to change the essence of my work life. I'll still teach. I'll still research and write. But my work won't be the be-all and end-all. Jake and our marriage-to-be have become my top priorities, and my work is becoming just one *part* of my life, not all of it—which, I'm now seeing, is a good thing; I feel much more balanced now, and much happier."

Three weeks before the trip to the beach, Jake had moved into Sarah's little town house with his ugly "guy" furniture and his black Lab, who shed hair everywhere. That day was one of the happiest in Sarah's life. She had no problem moving her flowered chintz settee so that in his La-Z-Boy he could have the best view of the TV; she wanted this to be his home, too, and she knew that little gesture would make him really happy. (She'd already upgraded her cable to get ESPN, much to his surprise and delight.) The day before, she had bought a new bed and water bowl for the dog, to welcome him into her home as well. When she saw Jake unpack his threadbare towels, she stopped him and chucked them into the garbage. "Let's use our wedding towels!" she said. Although Sarah herself hadn't moved, the arrival of Jake, his furniture, his dog, and the steady stream of wedding presents made her house feel like new to her. Her home instantly felt more alive and happier with Jake in it.

On the afternoon the invitations arrived, as Sarah moved between grading papers and mooning over the invitations, she realized that in the last few weeks she had stopped focusing on what she was giving up and ending to be married to Jake and had instead begun to connect with the joy of spending her life with him.

In the bridging stage of your engagement, you'll start to look with happiness and excitement to your future with your fiancé instead of being preoccupied with the past that you're leaving. Finally, after all the hard work of forming new relationships with yourself and others, you'll feel ready to cross the bridge into your new identity of married woman.

Ten days after the invitations arrived, Sarah and Jake sat at their dining-room table to address and stuff the envelopes. It was a long, slow process, and they took their time, knowing they'd never have this experience again in their lives. Both were lost in their own thoughts.

For Sarah, seeing her parents' name at the top of each of the 120 invitations brought home the fact that they were really giving her away, that her ties to her family were going to be forever altered as she and Jake became family on their wedding day. As she held their invitation in her hands, reflecting on its significance, she felt a roller coaster of emotions. First, she was sad, feeling a pit of grief in her stomach as she imagined letting go of her parents. Then she was angry with them. The fuller and richer her life had become with

Jake, the more she'd realized that there was a grimness and a joylessness to the work ethic her parents had pounded into her. Instead of staying stuck in feelings of resentment, though, Sarah pulled herself out by patting herself on the back: by choosing fun, athletic, nature-boy Jake instead of a straight-edged workaholic, Sarah had chosen a happier life for herself. The family she and Jake were going to create together would have a healthier balance of work and play.

As Sarah addressed each of the envelopes with the names of friends and loved ones, she went on a similar emotional ride, but one that, every time, reinforced how happy and excited she was to be marrying Jake.

Many brides-to-be describe their transitions out of the ending stage and into the bridging stage of their engagements like a fog finally lifting. For the early months of their engagement, they walked around consumed by feelings of loss and disorientation as they let go of old ways of being. They felt that the confusion would never end. They've been afraid that they'd be in a down, depressed funk on their wedding day, and that they'd never feel happy or excited about getting married, even though, deep down, they trusted that that was what they wanted to do. As the wedding approaches for these brides-to-be, however, joyful anticipation begins to creep back in.

Once you enter the bridging stage, you will have made the internal psychological adjustments necessary to begin your new life as a married woman. During this stage, women like Sarah, who've struggled with the loss of identity as a single woman or their single-minded focus on their careers, find themselves finally embracing how their fiancés enrich their lives. Brides-to-be who've had difficulty letting go of their dependence on their parents discover that they can be close with their families even as they put their fiancés first. Those who mourn the end of the days as boyfriend and girlfriend begin to see the richness and depth that come with making a lifelong commitment. And finally, women who are anxious about the state of their friendships with the girls reach a place of acceptance that, yes, things will change between them to a certain degree, but they're now more confident that things will work out for the best. In short, the confusion that accompanied all the many endings brides-to-be have faced is replaced with greater clarity, curiosity, and hope. The focus turns to the future.

Entering the bridging stage doesn't, however, mean that all the gray clouds will have permanently lifted, as Sarah discovered when she felt waves of sadness and anger while stuffing envelopes. But you'll likely find that, like Sarah, when the difficult emotions do arise, you will no longer stay stuck in a downward spiral. Instead, you'll embrace the emotions and feel them fully, and then they will quickly move on. On the whole, your positive feelings about your future with your fiancé will consistently outweigh your grief about the ending of your single life.

Bridging, then, is a time when the balance shifts, when your new life as a married woman begins to take shape in your mind, in your heart, and in your life. After all the hard work you will have done to end earlier chapters of your life, you'll begin to realize it all had a purpose.

Finally Feeling Ready

The bridging process that Carrie, the bride-to-be who survived real-estate hell with her fiancé, Alex (after freaking out about his credit-card debt), went through was reflected in the two very different experiences she had at the two bridal showers held in her honor.

As Carrie drove to her first shower, which was being thrown by her mother's friends, the primary emotion she felt was dread. Her mother's friends were quite a formidable group of ladies who were very vocal with their ideas of what's proper and what's not. To them, the idea of having a bridal shower too close to the wedding was outrageous. They pooh-poohed Carrie's request to schedule the party for one month before her big day. *The bed-and-bath shower*, the ladies decreed, *would be three months before Carrie and Alex walked down the aisle.* That's when it would be done, because that's when the ladies wanted it.

Although she and Alex had just made a down payment together, on the day of the shower, Carrie still wasn't feeling 100 percent ready to get married, as she had hoped she would be. Walking into the party, she felt like an imposter, like she was playing the role of the happy bride for her mom's friends. Privately, she was still in limbo, her feet still planted in the single world and her identity still in flux.

Feeling as ambivalent as she was about leaving her single life behind, it was hard for her to fully embrace the party atmosphere. "All these women, whom I'd known my whole life, had gathered to celebrate my wedding, and I felt like crawling under a rock," she told me. "I wanted to hide, and yet I had to be the center of attention. I was the bride, after all."

During the luncheon, Carrie gravitated toward an old family friend whose husband of forty years had just died. She had a long conversation with the widow. At her bridal shower, Carrie literally sat in a psychic field of grief, which reflected her contemplative, sad, inward focus much more accurately than the silly bridal-shower games she had to play.

Carrie pretended to bubble with excitement when it came time to open the gifts, thanking her mother's friends profusely as she opened each one so as not to seem rude or ungrateful. None of her mother's friends would have guessed that Carrie was still coming to terms with the endings in her life.

When her girlfriends threw her a kitchen shower two months later, Carrie was in a different place. As she and Alex had settled in to their new apartment, she'd begun to feel more settled in her new life with him. While she wasn't completely at home in her new house yet, daily life with him was becoming more and more natural. She felt more stable and solid than she had before, even though, truth be told, she was feeling a little gun-shy after what had happened at the last shower. "I was nervous that I'd want to hide again," she told me. "How sad would it be to miss out on this shower, too? I didn't want to have to pretend to be happy in front of twenty of my closest friends."

As she entered the friend's home where the shower was to take place, however, she found that she was much more relaxed. Slowly, she came out of hiding and began to step, however tentatively, into the role of happy bride. But this time she wasn't playing a role; she was genuinely happy.

When the poached salmon and spinach salad were cleared away, her friends gathered around her for the grand gift opening. This time, Carrie felt completely present, and a lot more comfortable. "I started opening presents—a silver colander, a Thanksgiving turkey platter, a baking dish—and I noticed how different this felt from the first shower," she told me. "At the first shower, I'd open a gift—monogrammed bath towels, say— and I'd gush and rave about how beautiful they were, but in my mind, I'd think, 'What's a single girl like me need all this stuff for?' or I'd resent the old lady who had foisted new initials and a new last name on me by monogramming the towels.

"At the kitchen shower, however, I didn't resent the gifts or question their purpose," she continued. "As I opened the mountain of presents, I began to see our married home and our married life take shape, and I could finally see myself in it with Alex."

It wasn't just the gifts that helped Carrie realize she was more ready for married life. It was the way she could hear, with new clarity and understanding, things that her friends were saying. With her single friends, she was able to hear for the first time how perfectly matched they thought she and Alex were, how genuinely happy they were for her, and how her relationship with Alex was one that many of them aspired to.

In chatting with her married friends, she felt like she was being welcomed into their world, "a married world that I didn't even know existed when I was single," she told me. "I heard stories about the challenges and unexpected pleasures of being newly married, about working through hard times together and feeling stronger as a couple for it. One friend talked about how her struggles with a nosy mother-in-law eventually helped her and her husband develop stronger boundaries and a stronger sense of themselves as a family. Another talked about how supported she felt by her husband during a difficult time in her career, and how that made her see the forever-ness of their marriage on a whole new level. Then there were the hilarious stories about living with a man twenty-four/seven—the different definitions of what a 'clean' kitchen is, the constant reminders that he needs to trim his nose hair, the epic struggles about asking for directions when they're lost. I guess I'd been hearing these stories all through the years, but I used to tune them out because they had no relevance to my life. Now, they had a whole new meaning and significance to me. They related directly to the life I was about to enter into."

Carrie's married friends asked her to tell their falling-in-love story, and they wanted to know more about the ins and outs of her relationship. "It was great," Carrie told me. "The way they were open about their marriages and the way they asked me about my marriage-to-be really helped me imagine my new role and life as a married woman." This is how bridging is experienced: all of a sudden you realize that something has begun to shift. Where you once reflected more on the past, now your inner gaze is more firmly fixed on the future.

As the bows and ribbons fell to the floor and the stories about marriage continued to be told, Carrie noticed that her single self—the identity to which she had been so attached—was now almost entirely in her past. The grueling work of grieving the endings was, for the most part, complete; she'd become vaguely aware of the shift in the preceding weeks, but at the shower, her readiness for marriage became apparent to her. The Carrie who opened and gushed over her friends' gifts was the new, about-to-be-married Carrie. At this shower, she had stopped fighting the change in identity. She felt ready to embrace her new life as a wife.

The Emotional To-Do List Item #11
On the Lookout for Bridge Moments

 Many brides-to-be don't notice they're in the bridging stage until it's been going on for a while.

As your wedding date approaches, keep an eye out for the moments when your new, married life feels more real to you than your old, single life. Bridge moments like this can be in-your-face, such as when the invitations arrived on Sarah's doorstep, or they can be more subtle, such as the way Carrie could hear—with new ears—her married friends' stories at her shower.

You may want to keep a running list of your bridge moments in your journal. That way, when your conflicted feelings resurface (as they occasionally will), you can refer to your list of bridge moments. Then you'll be able to see how far you've come from the grueling days of grief, and be aware of how ready you are, the majority of the time, to be married.

The Time for the Vows Is Now

"We've got to figure out the ceremony," Cynthia would say to Brian every few nights.

"I know, I know," Brian would always reply, shaking his head. "We've really got to do it."

Month after month, Cynthia and Brian, the couple who got engaged in the Alaskan wilderness, would have this same conversation. The ceremony—the whole reason for the reception, which was taking up all their time, energy, and concentration—had become just one more unfinished item on their long to-do list.

Foot-dragging about the ceremony may be more common than you think. I hear brides-to-be fret about it all the time. "It's the most meaningful and significant part of the wedding," Cynthia told me. "But we can't seem to focus on it. One of us really needs to lead the charge in planning it, but neither of us is willing to take the initiative."

Both Cynthia and Brian knew that their lack of focus on the ceremony didn't mean they shouldn't get married, and yet, they still couldn't get it done. The wedding planner kept dogging Cynthia with questions: Have you decided on your vows? The readings? The music?

"No," Cynthia replied each week. "But we'll get going on it this weekend, I promise."

One Saturday morning, Cynthia decided to keep her promise. She retrieved from the back of her wedding notebook the packet of readings their minister had given them at their last meeting. Brian put in the CD of the string quartet they'd hired, and with Vivaldi's *Four Seasons* playing in the background, the couple got down to work.

Brian opened the packet to a random page and started reading: "'You were born together, and together you shall be forevermore. You shall be together when the white wings of death scatter your days.'"

"'The white wings of death'?" Cynthia said. "Yikes. What's that from?"

"It's Kahlil Gibran, from *The Prophet*," replied Brian. "Definitely too airy-fairy for us."

"I'd say so," said Cynthia. "Keep reading."

"'Love is patient; love is kind; love is not envious or boastful or arrogant or rude,'" he said.

"I cannot do Corinthians!" Cynthia interrupted. "I just can't do it. I've heard it at so many weddings, it's become meaningless to me."

"Fine, fine," said Brian, starting to get a little frustrated. He scanned through the packet, searching for readings that were more "them." "What about this? 'Now you will feel no rain, for each of you will be shelter to the other,'" he read. "'Now you will feel no cold, for each of you will be warmth to the other.'"

"Oh, I like that!" Cynthia said. "Who is that?"

"It's an Apache wedding blessing," he replied. "It ends really nicely. Listen to this: 'Go now to your dwelling place to enter into the days of your togetherness. And may your days be good and long upon the earth.'"

"What do you think?" she said, hesitantly. "Do you like it?"

"Yeah," he replied. "What do you think?"

"Let me have a look," Cynthia said, taking the packet from Brian. "'Now there is no more loneliness, for each of you will be companion to the other,'" she read aloud, her voice catching in her throat. "'Now you are two persons, but there is one life before you.'" Tears trickled down Cynthia's face as she completed the blessing, and when she looked up at Brian, his eyes were watery, too. As they gazed into each other's teary eyes, what had initially been another annoying task to check off the to-do list had transformed into the most meaningful, moving, and intimate moment the two of them had shared in months.

"Oh my God," Brian said. "This is something we might actually read in our wedding ceremony. How amazing is that?"

"I know, I know," Cynthia replied. "We're doing it. We're really getting married!"

For the rest of the day, they felt a warmth and love for each other that they hadn't had complete access to for months, since both had been preoccupied with their individual internal emotions. After countless weeks of feeling somewhat separate, the bride- and groom-to-be were ready to come together, to look toward their future together. They were emotionally prepared to create their wedding ceremony, to put words to the very foundation of their marriage. As a couple, Cynthia and Brian were ready to cross the bridge into their new identities as husband and wife.

Often, your and your fiancé's ability and readiness to write the vows or plan the ceremony can be a good barometer of whether you've entered the bridging stage. Until both of you have completed your individual emotional work, trying to write your ceremony may feel unnatural, premature, or forced. The words will not come easily; you won't quite know what you want to say to each other. This is because you are still in the ending stage, and the psychological work at this stage can be all-consuming. And that can make thinking about your future difficult, if not impossible.

As you pass through the ending stage and into the bridging stage, you and your fiancé will likely become interested in your ceremony. This will occur naturally. With the invitations in the mail and the reply cards starting to trickle in, your wedding and your future together will become more concrete in your minds. When the time is right, you'll feel not only ready, but most likely *eager*, to find just the right words and readings to embody your feelings for each other.

Being Mindful with the Mindless Details

Bridging is marked by your newfound ability to reflect and imagine your marriage calmly, even joyfully. For many brides-to-be, the small details involved with the wedding provide a focus for their reflection.

As your wedding day approaches, there will be a million and one tiny tasks that you need to complete before you walk down the aisle: confirm the limos; gather your jewelry, panty hose, and clear nail polish (in case your stockings run); pack for your honeymoon. Some tasks require more attention and care than others. When writing checks, you need to keep a clear head so you don't accidentally add an extra zero and end up paying the DJ eight thousand dollars instead of eight hundred for playing "I Had the Time of My Life" at just the right moment. But slipping treats like bottles of water, cookies, and chocolates into the welcome baskets or folding programs isn't quite as demanding, and many brides-to-be cherish these solitary moments. Taking care of these small tasks can provide a quiet time for you to reflect on the journey you've taken, as well as what comes next.

Maria, the bride-to-be who feared her wedding would cause her family to fall apart, had a complete turnaround once she figured out what had plagued her. Released from her worries about her family, Maria fell in love with the crafty aspects of her wedding. She taught herself calligraphy and addressed the invitations herself. She dried rose petals for her flower girls' baskets. She designed and sewed her own veil. And two weeks before her June wedding, Maria took on the daunting task of handcrafting 120 favors. She painted terra-cotta flowerpots, filled them with dirt, planted alyssum (a dainty, tiny lavender flower) in them, and tied a bow around each one. The project was time consuming, but she loved doing it.

As Maria sat at a picnic table in her parents' backyard and spent hour after hour by herself, painting and planting, her mind was quiet, "which was a miracle after being so agitated during most of the engagement," she told me during a phone call shortly after her wedding. "Painting the flowerpots turned out to be a kind of meditation," she remembered. "I thought a lot about where I'd been as a single woman, how my relationship with my family was changing, and what kind of marriage Jeff and I would have. Over time, I began to view each flowerpot as a symbol of our marriage-to-be—a living, delicate being, full of new life. I loved that I was giving this symbolic gift to our guests, all of whom had given me so much. I loved that they were taking a symbol of our marriage home with them."

Meanwhile, Pauline, who had worked hard to preserve her relationships with her four best single girlfriends, became obsessed with place cards. She felt that plain white place cards were too blah, and yet all the fancy flowered ones were too formal. In the weeks leading up to her wedding, she scoured every party and paper store in a twenty-mile radius, in search of what, she wasn't quite sure.

And then she found them: simple white place cards with a light green border, a perfect fit for her springtime wedding. She was elated — almost too elated, she told me, since she isn't prone to precision like that, especially when it comes to minutiae like the border on a place card. Since this single-minded focus on this one item was so out of character, I asked her to explore the meaning behind it.

"I don't think it has any meaning," she told me. "It's just some weird obsession I had."

Not necessarily, I told her. I asked her to think about why, out of all the details that go into planning a wedding, she had focused on place cards. Why not her shoes? Or the wedding programs? Why not the welcome baskets or her bouquet? "What," I asked her, "do place cards mean to you?"

"Well, it's pretty basic," she said. "Place cards tell the guests where to sit."

"Okay," I said. "So why is it so important to you where your guests sit?"

Pauline told me that when she had gone out on her many quests for the perfect place cards, she had daydreamed about her wedding. She imagined herself in her strapless wedding dress, hugging, kissing, and greeting her eighty guests. She reflected on her relationships with them. She thought about who she'd seat at each round table of eight. And she was particularly concerned with where to place her four best single girlfriends, whose reactions to her engagement and marriage-to-be had consumed much of her emotional energy since she got engaged.

"Hmm," she said, beginning to process this new perspective. "Maybe focusing on place cards—on where my single friends are going to sit at my wedding—is a way for me to figure out how to place them, so to speak, in my new life as a wife."

With that insight, Pauline had discovered the meaning in her odd obsession with place cards. She chose to focus on place cards—not the boutonnieres, not the ceremony music—because place cards kept Pauline engaged in the psychological process of reworking and redefining her friendships with her single girlfriends.

To outsiders, a bride-to-be's strange obsession with, say, green-bordered place cards, sachets of rice and dried flowers, or her shoes—which no one will see under the big white dress—may seem like just one more indication that she has gone off the deep end into the world of the picky and entitled. Many brides-to-be are teased or ridiculed by friends and family for caring far too much about seemingly inconsequential details; others simply feel embarrassed by their new, compulsive behavior. For these reasons, most engaged women hide these odd behaviors; they keep them quiet. Some, like Pauline, sneak out to every paper and party store in town without telling a soul.

If you buy into what your friends or family (or society)

say and write off your odd fixation to "crazy bride behavior," you're missing out on opening a window into what might be still happening for you, psychologically. As Maria's and Pauline's stories demonstrate, there's meaning to be found in your particular obsession—you just have to think of it metaphorically. Ask yourself: Why am I devoting so much effort and energy to this one random thing? Why *this* wedding detail and not all the others?

Here's one more example. After Cynthia and Brian spent a romantic week writing their wedding ceremony and falling in love with each other all over again, Cynthia slipped back into manic-woman mode to get the programs written and printed. They were having three hundred guests at their wedding—a huge affair—and she wanted each program to be tied with a blue gingham bow. And she insisted that she do it all by herself.

The problem was, there were simply too many bows and too little time. Cynthia was tying bows up to the moment she put on her wedding dress.

When she told me this story after her wedding, I asked her point-blank: What was up with all the bows? Why couldn't she delegate the task to someone a little less busy than she? Why was it important to tie all the bows herself? In short, what did the bows mean, metaphorically, to Cynthia?

"I really can't explain it," she told me. "The programs were my babies. Maybe I was tying up loose ends in my life? Maybe it was a way for me to *literally* put a knot on, to close up, my single life. This I do know: when I finally handed the bag of finished programs to my brother to take to the church,

I felt really psyched and totally ready to get married." For the final two months of her engagement, Cynthia had been moving toward her new, married life. But before she could fully embrace it, it was as if she had to tie up her single life with a blue gingham bow, a rather apt metaphor for the whole bridging process.

The Emotional To-Do List Item #12
Your Secret Wedding Obsessions

 What's your equivalent of the perfect place card or the blue gingham bow? What wedding detail are you particularly obsessed with getting just right? (Hint: you probably haven't admitted it to anyone for fear that you may sound like a wedding-obsessed bridezilla.)

To find the metaphor in your secret tiny detail, dissect it. Consider what the detail itself means (place cards as a way of not only seating people at your wedding but, metaphorically, of finding a place for them in your married life). Think about the physical act of getting the detail just right (what does tying three hundred bows mean, metaphorically?). Explore what it tells you about what you're engaged in psychologically (are you tying up loose ends, or reworking friendships?). Finally, reflect on how it's helping you get what you need emotionally (grounding yourself by working with plants and potting soil) and how it's helping you transition into your future.

CHAPTER 8

The Big Day
Being an Emotionally Engaged Bride

You Can Plan Almost Everything . . .

Y ou can spend months—years, even—planning your wedding down to the last second. You can specify the arrival of the fleet of limos to the minute, the placement of the grooms-men to the inch, and the precise time you'll cut the cake.

But you can't orchestrate the moments that will make your wedding unique, memorable, and yours. You can't plan, for example, how, as you and your dad regally make your way down the aisle, your cathedral-length veil catches on a pew, causing you both to be yanked backward and then crack up in laughter, lightening the mood. How your tough-guy fiancé becomes a puddle as you approach him in your big white dress. How your ring bearer stumbles on his way up to the altar. You can't plan for these real, authentic moments. They just happen, and your job as the bride is to allow for them and, more importantly, to enjoy them as they're happening.

The same goes for your emotions. You can't predict or control how you're going to feel on your wedding day. (Remember how you assumed your engagement would be the happiest time of your life?) All you can really do is enjoy the ride.

Your wedding will likely be one of the most magnificent, glorious, and joyful events of your life. It is, after all, the day you've been completely focused on for the last many months (or, perhaps, since you were five years old); it has likely gotten more attention and energy, both in preparation and emotion, than any other day of your life. On your wedding day, in addition to throwing the biggest party of your life, you cross the bridge into your new identity as a married woman, entering the new and unknown world that is married life.

After the wedding invitations arrived, Sarah coasted along for a few weeks feeling happy. But as her wedding day approached, she started to ping-pong between two emotions. On one hand, she was excited that she finally felt ready to marry Jake. On the other, the predominant emotion she felt was anxiety: Sarah was very anxious about the walk down the aisle.

Each week in our individual counseling sessions, Sarah would bring up two or three reasons why it made perfect sense that she was a nervous wreck about walking down the aisle:

"It's such a grand entrance," she said one week. "What if I trip?"

"It's silent," she said the next week. "What if I get the giggles?"

The week before her wedding, her list grew tenfold: "It's ceremonial: my guests will rise to honor me. It's sad: my dad's going to be a weepy mess. It's happy: Jake's going to be ecstatic. It's epic and ancient: think about the billions of brides who've walked this walk before me. It's preserved for posterity: it will be the most photographed walk of my life."

"You're right," I said to her at our final session before her big day. "It's nothing short of life-changing: on the way down the aisle, you'll be single, and on the way up, you'll be married. It's during your wedding ceremony that you make the transition into your new identity and life."

"So, don't be nervous?" she responded. "Yeah, right!"

"Believe me, Sarah, I understand where you're coming from," I told her. "It *is* the biggest walk of your life. My question to you, however, is this: How do you know—*today*, two weeks before your wedding—that you'll be a nervous wreck walking down the aisle fourteen days from now?"

"I don't," she replied. "But I'm pretty sure I'm going to be anxious."

"Okay, but you can't be certain," I told her. "What if, instead of convincing yourself that you'll be nervous just before your ceremony, you tell yourself that you will simply be *curious* about what you're feeling? What if you make a conscious effort to let in whatever feelings arise, let them course through your body and your mind? What if you treat the feelings you have when you walk down the aisle the same way you did when you were stuffing the envelopes? That day, you let yourself feel the pang of sadness about leaving your family, but then a feeling of happiness about marrying Jake quickly followed. Remember that? What if you let one feeling flow through to the next, and let yourself be where you are?"

"I guess I could *try* that approach," Sarah said, sounding unconvinced. "But I still think I'm going to be a wreck. I mean, the ceremony's where it all happens!"

"That's true," I said. "But do you want to be so wrapped up in your nerves that you miss it?"

"Fine, fine," she sighed. "I'll let you know how it goes."

A week after her honeymoon, Sarah called me with a full report. "I woke up on my wedding day feeling oddly relaxed," she told me. "I waited for the nerves to kick in and take over, but they didn't.

"I replayed in my mind what you said to me: 'Don't push my emotions away. Feel them. Let them flow through me, one after the other after the other.' I was on the lookout for nervousness, but all I genuinely felt was excitement! I couldn't believe it!"

By the time the limousine pulled into her parents' driveway to take them to the church, Sarah was ready to jump out of her skin. "Let's go, let's go! I'm ready," Sarah told her maid of honor, who had known about the struggles and sadness she had experienced during her engagement. After spending nearly ten months wishing she felt happy and worrying about feeling nervous, Sarah had arrived. She didn't want to wait another minute to marry Jake.

"Walking down the aisle, I was happy and bawling at the same time, and it was perfect," she remembered. "The simultaneous crying and smiling completely reflected how I was feeling. I was sad *and* excited *and*, yes, a little nervous, but by the time I reached Jake, I was happy and surprisingly calm."

During the ceremony, Sarah was stunned to find herself

feeling almost casual, which she never could have predicted. She felt connected to Jake and connected to herself. Her feet were on the ground, and she was present with what was happening to her and to them. Her smile was easy and natural. She waved to friends and family from the altar. "After all those months of being nervous and upset, there I was, getting married and feeling completely at home doing it," she said. "Mainly, I was just so excited to be up at the altar—a feeling I never thought I'd have, even two days ago."

Sarah was able to let go of her preconceived idea that she would be overcome with nervousness walking down the aisle, and as a result, she felt whatever emotions arose, naturally and authentically. She didn't fight her excitement, even though it didn't fit her picture of what she'd be like on her wedding day. She didn't try to suppress her tears as she walked down the aisle, nor the huge smile that illuminated her face as the tears flowed. Sarah let her mixed bag of emotions run through her, and her experience at the altar was more real, connected, peaceful, and fun than she ever imagined it could be.

Clinging to Your Vision

Some brides are so eager to feel the transformation going on inside them and in their lives that they end up squeezing the life and spirit out of their wedding ceremonies. When you have an agenda like this—when you need yourself to feel a certain way—you undermine the possibility for the surfacing of authentic feeling.

This is exactly what happened to Tracy, the bride who re-grieved her mother's death during her engagement. After spending so much of her engagement feeling sad and angry and lonely, she was tired of being in a dark place. "I felt like I'd done my emotional work really well," she told me after the wedding, "and I thought I deserved a huge payoff, a prize, for putting in the time." In Tracy's mind, her prize was to feel like the earth moved when she got married. "I wanted fireworks to go off inside of me, signaling I'd changed."

The mood during their ceremony wasn't somber, as she had expected. The rose ritual honoring her mother turned out to be uplifting, as she and her family members remembered her mother fondly and felt her presence in the beautiful day she brought for her daughter. The tone of the entire ceremony stayed in this vein; it was light and fun and full of laughter. Tracy and her fiancé wanted to honor the merging of their two families, so at the altar they lined up three vases—one representing her family, one for his family, and one for their new, little family. As the bride and groom removed a daisy from each of their family's respective vases, the table shook, causing all three vases to tip over with a bang. Not once, not twice, but three times one vase or another tipped over, and with each tipped vase, the laughter between them and among their gathered guests grew louder and louder. It was a silly, unpredictable, absurd moment, sure to be remembered for years to come.

When the vases steadied and it was time for the couple to be pronounced husband and wife, Tracy was poised. "I was happy and calm, but I kept scanning my emotions and my body to see if anything major was happening, if anything essential was changing within me," she said. "But nothing really did. I ended up feeling disappointed that the earth didn't move the second I said 'I do.'"

Tracy wanted so much to feel something profound happen that she wasn't engaged in what was really happening emotionally during the ceremony. She was trying to fit her experience of getting married into what she thought it *should* be, rather than just letting it be what it was. In looking for the one big emotion, she couldn't experience the many different shades of emotions that ran through her. Tracy wasn't *in* the moment; she was *observing* herself in it. She was a witness to her wedding ceremony, rather than a participant in it.

If I Knew *Then* What I Know *Now* . . .

I thought that Rick and I were going to avoid wedding-day jitters because we had the smallest, most low-key wedding possible—it was just the two of us, our pastor, and a photographer, beside a creek in Colorado. But just before we got out of the car to hike to the ceremony site, my fiancé and I were gripped with nerves and struck down with upset stomachs. Luckily, we had Pepto-Bismol in the glove compartment, and we each did a shot!

On our brief hike to the site, we cracked up about the ridiculousness of the situation—how we both had to coat our stomachs before saying "I do." But I think the laughing really helped us get the kinks out. When we arrived at the site, the pastor was waiting for us, and we were both fully present and engaged with what was about to take place. Our ceremony was intensely intimate, and getting married in nature was so powerful and peaceful. Our walk back to the car was quiet and reflective. The whole experience was amazing, but how could we have predicted the Pepto?

—*Gillian, married nine months*

Being a "Zen Bride"

Pauline, who had been concerned about the state of her friendships during her engagement, was able to make a shift in attitude by the time her wedding day arrived. She felt confident about the emotional work she'd done during her engagement; she had done the best she could to preserve her friendships, and she felt both calm and curious about what the future would hold for her and her single friends. She was prepared for what was to come next: married life. In fact, once she purchased her green-bordered place cards, it was all systems go, and she was ready to walk down the aisle. "It's awful to say this, but I'd put so much time and energy into planning our wedding that part of me just wanted to get it over with," she told me. "I was tired of talking about it and thinking about it. I wanted my life back.

"I always thought that on our wedding day, I'd feel and behave like I did at our engagement party: excited and revved up, giddy and loud and ebullient," she told me. "After all the work that went into both my engagement and the wedding, I was looking forward to kicking up my heels and just having fun."

When the spring weekend at a country inn in Virginia finally arrived, however, Pauline was surprised that she wasn't bouncing off the walls. She was more grounded than she had anticipated, and she was in a soulful, deep place. What was unusual was that she didn't fight her mood; she let herself feel solemn, despite the fact that she had expected to be in party mode when her wedding finally arrived.

"I called myself the 'Zen bride,'" she told me after the wedding, "and being Zen turned out to be the best wedding present I could have given to myself."

When I asked her what she meant, she explained that a Zen bride is, well, Zen, living in the present moment. She has let go of all preconceived ideas about how she should feel during her ceremony and reception. Any bride can be a Zen bride, because being a Zen bride means, simply, abandoning whatever agenda she may have for herself. If she had hoped to be calm and peaceful but she feels jittery, that's okay with her. If she expected to feel sad walking on her dad's arm down the aisle but her true feeling is excitement, all the better.

Do you have to have a Zen-like and emotionally easygoing engagement to be a Zen bride? Not at all. Nor do you have to study, practice, meditate, or utter a single "Om." All you need to do is detach from your expectations and be, simply, where you are.

By allowing herself to experience whatever emotion— even seriousness—she was feeling in the moment, Pauline also felt a sense of aliveness and connection to herself. She didn't try to resurrect the party girl in her; she let herself be where she was. And it's in these feelings of aliveness and connection that true, real, authentic happiness lies.

"During the ceremony, I felt joyful, but very serious," she said. "I was a teary bride. I really thought about what I was saying, what was happening, and I worked hard to be really present.

"When I said my vows—especially 'to have and to hold from this day forward' and 'in sickness and in health'—the meaning of the words hit me like a ton of bricks. Drew and I had gone over the ceremony a million times, but saying the vows directly to him, before the priest, God, and my family and friends, was so intense. I was really pledging the rest of my life to Drew, and I was taking on the responsibility of his life. At that moment, it truly felt like an honor to become his wife. It was all very solemn for me."

To her surprise, Pauline's ceremony was far more than just a precursor to the big party she had spent so many months planning. As she said her vows—as she crossed the bridge into her new identity as a married woman—she connected with the profundity of the moment in a way she hadn't expected. The ceremony turned out to be far more powerful than she had imagined, and she was far more moved by it than she'd anticipated.

"Right after the ceremony, everyone rushed to congratulate us, and I felt like I was shot out of a cannon," she said. "At that moment, I wished we could have jumped into a limo to go to the reception, instead of just walking across a lawn."

After greeting a few guests, and with no limo at their disposal, Pauline grabbed her new husband by the hand and dragged him across the lawn and into the ladies' room inside the inn. (Her brand-new husband wisely didn't protest too loudly.) She needed time, just the two of them, to absorb what they'd gone through. She didn't want that intimate, life-changing moment between them to flame out so quickly. "I needed to create a break between that intense experience and the party and music and people coming up to me," she told me.

After a few minutes of staring into each other's eyes in the ladies' room and replaying their different experiences during the ceremony, Pauline washed her tearstained face and reapplied her lipstick. She was ready to face the string quartet's cocktail music. Later, as she and Drew posed for formal photos with their wedding party, Pauline became overjoyed and giddy, even more than at the engagement party, since now her transition from single to married was complete. It was done. All she had to do was celebrate, and she soon found that the celebration felt even more meaningful to her after having been so deeply moved by the ceremony. "I had just married the man I love, and I was surrounded by everyone in the world I love," she recounted. "I was so happy that I was literally jumping up and down for joy! The photographer kept scolding me to stand still, but I couldn't. It was just too great a moment in my life!"

After the photos, Pauline bustled the train of her gown, removed her veil, grabbed glasses of champagne for Drew and herself, and joined in the fun. She threw herself into her party—eating the great food, dancing with her new husband, and visiting with relatives she hadn't seen in years. She also made a point of stepping back occasionally to observe what was going on around her, and she was amused and delighted by what she saw: Drew's grandfather and her aunt were dancing together. Their two sets of friends were mingling (some getting a little closer than others—maybe another wedding would come out of hers?). The guest book was filling. The floral centerpieces were prettier and more dramatic than she could ever have hoped. And the simple green-bordered place cards looked just right.

"I had my fairy-tale wedding," she said, "and because I was a Zen bride and let myself feel whatever I felt during the ceremony, it was so much more meaningful than just a simple fairy tale."

The Emotional To-Do List Item #13
What You "Should" Feel

 The more you articulate your emotional agenda for yourself on your wedding day, the easier it will be to let go of it. In your journal, write as much as you can about your preconceived ideas, fantasies, and images about what you "should" feel before you walk down the aisle; during your walk down the aisle; during the ceremony and the reception; and afterward, in the honeymoon suite.

Now your job is to let go of these images and ideas. What can you do to be fully in the moment, and to experience authentically whatever emotions you have? Try creating a mantra for yourself ("Be where I am," or "*Que sera, sera*," or "Let 'em rip!") that you can repeat in your mind. What else can you do to help yourself be in the moment on your wedding day so you can experience your full range of emotions?

Embracing Bride Brain

Now that you know what your wedding-day goal is—to be in the moment, to feel whatever it is you're feeling—take the following to heart: nobody—not even Zen masters—can be fully present every single minute of the day. And certainly not a bride on her wedding day. Thus, an important aspect of being an in-the-moment Zen bride is to accept those times when you're not.

Carrie had 290 guests at a four-star hotel in San Francisco, with white-gloved waiters and hot-and-cold running champagne, yet she was still able to remain, for the most part, connected to herself the day she married Alex. "Our wedding day was like a dream sequence," she later told me. "Some moments were really clear to me, and others were really blurry. Our whole wedding day was like that: clear, blurry, clear, blurry."

During the clear moments, Carrie described feeling more alert and alive than she ever had. She was emotionally present and completely aware of what was happening and how she was feeling: the weepiness, jumpiness, and short-temperedness she felt during the hours leading up to the wedding. The frustration and anger she felt when her mom criticized her earrings as "too big" just moments before the photographer arrived to take her portrait (and the brief, hurt outburst of tears and screams that followed). The tenderness she felt as she held her five-year-old nephew's hand before the processional. The gratitude and warmth she felt for her battalion of bridesmaids. The flood of love she felt for her parents moments before walking down the aisle. The pit of sadness in her stomach as she realized she was making the final break from her family. The rush of excitement and eagerness she felt as she took Alex's hand to walk up to the altar. The little-girl giggles she got during the ceremony when she looked out and saw her two brothers smiling, winking, and making faces at her. The annoyance with herself for spacing out during the readings. The sober intensity she felt as they said their vows. The elation and joy of walking back down the aisle as a married couple.

Whew. That's a lot of emotions for one bride to have in a half-hour wedding ceremony, and the reception hadn't even started yet.

Then there were the other, brief moments when Carrie checked out emotionally. "I didn't expect to feel as many different emotions as I did on my wedding day," Carrie told me. "Sometimes, I'd get completely overwhelmed, so I'd detach from feeling anything." For Carrie, detaching from her emotions—letting things get blurry and not being in the moment—was an effective and impromptu coping mechanism. When she detached, she could regroup, refocus, reengage with what was happening, and reconnect to what she was feeling. Letting herself be out of the moment for a little while actually helped her then get back into it when she was ready.

Carrie's occasional detachment was similar to Pauline's dragging her brand-new husband into the ladies' room, in that it created a breather and a buffer, an opportunity to slow down the rush of heightened emotions. Carrie, however, chose to make the break while staying at the party; she did it within herself.

She'd seen it happen to other friends on their wedding days. One minute, Carrie would be talking with the bride, who was chatty and lighthearted. The next minute, the bride would be mute and have a far-off look in her eyes. The bride wouldn't stay wordless for long, but in that brief moment, she disappeared within herself.

I call this phenomenon "Bride Brain," or the momentary zone-out that envelops many brides on their wedding days. Why does Bride Brain happen? Well, weddings are an intensely *private* experience for you and your fiancé, but, at the same time, they are a *public* event. All eyes are on you (in Carrie and Alex's case, 290 pairs of eyes), watching closely as you commit the intimate act of joining together for the rest of your lives. Switching gears from one intense *internal* emotional experience to another intense *external* experience of, say, chatting with a guest can feel like emotional whiplash. Bride Brain provides a reprieve, a resting place, an escape, an opportunity to move from one emotional space to another. It helps you manage the interplay between the public and the private.

Carrie and Alex sat at their tiny table for two during dinner in the hotel ballroom, and the blurry-clear cycle continued. Some moments Carrie would be enraptured with Alex, holding his hand, admiring his sparkling new wedding band. Other times, she'd look across the ballroom at a table of single friends, watching their flirtatious fun and feeling a mild pang that she'd never sit at the singles' table again. Chatting with her parents' best friends, Carrie often slipped into Bride Brain, using the comfortable conversation with people she'd known her whole life as a brief vacation from all the emotion. Watching her parents dance like crazy teenagers, big broad smiles on their faces expressing their happiness, was a clear point that connected Carrie to her own joy. At the end of the night, Carrie and Alex walked slowly, hand in hand, to the honeymoon suite, exhausted and in awe of what they had just experienced together.

Carrie didn't judge herself for spacing out into Bride Brain; she let it happen, and she accepted it. "I took in a lot of what happened on our wedding day," she told me. "And frankly, I'm not sure I could have taken in much more. I needed those little breaks; they made it possible for me to be as present as I was."

How to Be Emotionally Engaged on Your Wedding Day

One reason it's called your "big day" is because of the supersized emotions you'll probably feel. Here are some tips (several of which sum up what we've discussed in this chapter) that can help you stay connected to yourself, feel your emotions as they're happening, and be present on your wedding day. Keep these tips in mind and, hopefully, you won't have to watch your wedding day on video when you return from your honeymoon just to remember what happened.

1. *Breathe.* If you're not breathing, you're probably not feeling.

2. *Let yourself feel whatever you feel.* This is the goal. You won't be able to predict your emotional state that day, so all you can prepare for is lots of feelings. The key is to let the feelings flow through you, one after another.

3. *Accept that sometimes you won't be in the moment.* Allow yourself to have moments of Bride Brain in which you regroup and reconnect to yourself. Zone out and disappear into yourself, or escape to the ladies' room to steal a quick moment alone. If you take a break from the emotional intensity from time to time, you'll be able to jump back in and be fully present when you are ready.

4. *Connect with your brand-new husband.* In the middle of the reception, stop. Take a few moments, just the two of you. Focus on each other. Gaze into each other's eyes. Feel the fullness of your love, the wonder of what you're going through together. All the wedding hoopla is about your union, so feel united!

5. *Slow down.* It's your day. Step back, look around the church, the temple, the reception hall, the room. Enjoy the fruits of your labors—the hand-painted flowerpots, the blue gingham bows. Taste the food. Drink the champagne. Visit with guests who've flown in from afar. Be a guest at your own wedding.

6. *Let go of perfectionism.* Do whatever advance planning you need to, but when the big day arrives, let your wedding be what it wants to be. An event like this will have its

own personality, rhythm, and soul. Magical, intangible elements can't be planned (and you wouldn't want them to be). They just happen, so make room for the unexpected.

7. *Be delighted by spontaneity.* Carrie and Alex gave their band a strict list of "Do Not Play" songs. As they went to cut the cake, however, a drippy solo saxophone began warbling. "Oh my God, is that Kenny G?" Carrie gasped, horrified. It was. Today, the photos and the memories of cutting the cake to the cheesy Kenny G song are some of their most treasured, charming, and beloved. "We would *never* have planned to have Kenny G serenade us as we cut the cake," Carrie told me. *"Believe me.* But in a funny way, we're so happy it happened."

CHAPTER 9

After the Wedding
Honeymoon and First Year

Honeymoon Hiatus

It's over. The wedding you planned, dreamed of, and stressed about for months has come and gone. Now it's just the two of you, on your honeymoon. Out of the spotlight of being bride and groom, your honeymoon is time for R&R and umbrella drinks, a time to relax and have fun. You'll experience the new joy of being husband and wife, but even in paradise you may hit some minor bumps in the road if you're not prepared for them.

Two days after their wedding in Virginia, Pauline and Drew flew to Hawaii. The first morning they woke up in their high-rise hotel overlooking Waikiki, Pauline noticed how different it already felt to be married. "It was romantic and fun to roll over and say, 'Good morning, husband,' but that's not what I'm talking about," she told me. "I couldn't believe I was so happy about *not* being a bride anymore! Without a wedding to stress about, and lists and tasks and things to do, I was free to think about whatever I wanted. My brainpower expanded by fifty percent overnight. I didn't have to worry about fitting into my dress anymore, so I could eat and drink whatever I wanted. I had pancakes and bacon, beer at lunch, and wine at dinner. French fries between meals, even! After eight months of being so focused on the wedding, it was great to finally relax about everything."

Physically, mentally, and emotionally bone-tired from their wedding, Pauline and Drew settled into a slow-paced honeymoon routine. The days began leisurely, with snuggly mornings in bed followed by chowing down at the breakfast buffet. Then they'd head to the beach, where they'd park themselves under an umbrella for the rest of the day. They'd read, rest, swim, sun, relax, and talk about their wedding for hours on end, discussing details from the macro—"Wasn't it amazing how much everybody danced?"—to the micro— "Do you think your mom liked her nosegay?" Lazy afternoons they'd spend walking the beach or watching TV, napping, or, more often, consummating their marriage in the cool of their air-conditioned suite. Then they'd dress up for dinner in the fancy hotel dining room, where they'd dance between courses to the piano music, just as newlyweds should. Pauline thought they were doing their honeymoon just right.

After four days of this mellow routine, though, Pauline noticed herself getting agitated. "I felt a lot of pressure to be gaga over Drew every second and to have great sex every single day, maybe even twice a day," she explained. "I started worrying: Are we being as romantic as we should be? Are our conversations as deep as they should be?"

Pauline had run smack into the challenge honeymooning couples often face: their expectations of what a honeymoon should be. We *should* be locked in our hotel room 24/7, ordering room service because we can't get out of bed. We *should* be constantly rehashing and reliving our wedding, detailing every second and minute. We *should* be having deep, meaningful, profound conversations all the time about our relationship and future. We *should* be walking the beaches hand in hand, dewy-eyed and mooning over each other. We *should* be relaxed. We *should* try new things like snorkeling, deep-sea diving, waterskiing, windsurfing, parasailing, hiking, golfing, and bungee jumping. The problem is, all these "shoulds" put pressure on you to conform to some cinematic image of what a honeymoon is. And that sets you up for disappointment when things don't measure up.

A honeymoon is part fantasy and part reality, but nobody likes to account for the "reality" aspect of it. The fantasy is easy to grab on to: after the whirlwind of the wedding, the two of you are whisked off to an exotic locale for intense one-on-one time. You practice calling each other "husband" and "wife" in a gorgeous setting. You have no agenda beyond relaxing and loving each other. With no work, responsibilities, family, friends, to-do lists, or wedding stress on your honeymoon, your job is to let a curtain of privacy fall around you and drink each other in.

Reality, however, doesn't take a vacation just because you're on your honeymoon. You may be tired and drained from the wedding. You and your husband may have different definitions of "fun" and "relaxation" that don't fit together perfectly. You may think you and your new husband are not acting romantic or sexy enough. If so, don't force yourself to feel something you don't; just feel whatever it is you're feeling. And cut yourself a lot of slack. This is a time for R&R— that's rest and relaxation, not recrimination and regret.

Pauline told me that she fretted in silence about their honeymoon for an entire day. "I worried that we weren't doing it 'right,'" she said. "But then I looked over at my husband, who was so content to be rubbing my feet and reading his book under our beach umbrella, and I realized I was asking too much of us. Wanting fourteen days and nights of deep conversation and mind-blowing sex is unrealistic. What we needed was to be together and do whatever we felt like doing."

When it dawned on her that they'd never have a honeymoon again, Pauline snapped out of her angst. "I could either continue to make up reasons why we were failing some imaginary honeymoon test, or I could stop worrying and join my happy husband," she said. "I chose to relax, and that's when I started to feel happier. And sexier, too. Strange, huh?"

Not at all. When Pauline let go of her preconceived ideas about what her honeymoon should be, she could be fully present with her husband under the umbrella at Waikiki. It was at that point that his foot rub stopped being simply soothing and became foreplay.

The Emotional To-Do List Item #14
What "Should" Your Honeymoon Be Like?

Before your wedding, take some time to explore your ideas and images of what makes a "perfect" honeymoon. How has this image been influenced by pop culture (TV and movies), stories from family and friends, and cultural myths and traditions (such as never leaving the bedroom)?

What are your expectations for your own honeymoon? What do you expect of yourself? Of your new husband? Of your relationship? Of your sex life? Of your destination? Of the weather? Of your activities? In other words, what ideas of "perfection" do you harbor for your honeymoon?

Then, consider this: What if you're tired when your plane lands? What if it rains? Can your honeymoon withstand all your expectations, or are you setting yourself up for disappointment during those moments when you're inevitably tired, cranky, and feeling less romantic or deep than you think you should be? Can you let go of your agenda for your honeymoon and enjoy it for what it is?

The Newlywed Cocoon

In my experience, many newlyweds feel conflicted about coming home from their honeymoons. On one hand, they're eager and excited to get home and settle into married life. On the other, after being the bride and groom, up on a pedestal and at the center of attention for so many months, it can feel anticlimactic to unpack your bags, watch your tans fade, and get back to humdrum everyday life. Some newlyweds even go through wedding withdrawal; postwedding life can seem flat, dull, and empty. After months of filling every spare second stressing about the wedding, checking off the to-do list, or going to parties thrown in your honor, many newlyweds find themselves staring at each other, thinking, "Okay, what do we do now?"

This lack of attention and lack of things to do may initially feel like a void in your life—and your instincts may be to fill that void and keep yourselves busy. After a few quiet nights at home, just the two of you, you may reach for the phone to make plans to fill your calendar.

Not so fast, newlyweds. If you pack the days, nights, and weekends immediately following your wedding or honeymoon with social events, you're avoiding the void, not accepting it for what it is. In order to have an emotionally engaged marriage, you must let in the moments of quiet, inactivity, and stillness, because that's when it's easiest to connect authentically, not only to yourself and to your new identity, but to each other. In other words, spending a lazy Sunday afternoon reading the newspaper together on the couch facilitates getting to know each other as husband and wife more than a Sunday packed with brunch with one couple, tennis with another, and dinner at his parents' house.

When newlyweds give themselves space, time, and privacy to simply be together, a cocoon often builds up around them in their first months of marriage, and many newlyweds report an igniting of grand passions between them. Having made a lifelong commitment to each other, you may experience new and deeper feelings of connection—engulfing, crazy-in-love, bordering-on-obsession engrossment with your spouse. (The long-term commitment place in your brain may be lighting up like a pinball machine.) Day by married day, the high of the wedding grows into deeper, stronger, and steadier feelings of family and forever. Cocooned together in your new, married life, you're oblivious to and uninterested in the world around you.

Believe it or not, there is a purpose to all this passion. By tuning out the world and focusing so intensely on each other, you're getting to know each other in your new roles as husband and wife, which helps to build the foundation of your family.

After your wedding, you're still bridging into your new identities. Obviously, neither of you is single anymore. Nor, however, are you completely at home in your new roles and identities of "husband" and "wife." In fact, you're complete beginners. You're on the bunny slope of marriage, and it takes a year to eighteen months or sometimes even longer of being married, of being a wife, before you find your natural rhythm. The key is to allow yourself to learn.

How a Marriage Grows

You both come into your marriage with disparate histories, different ideas of what's right and wrong, and strong convictions on how things should be done. Your job, as a married couple, is to create together a new reality that accommodates, respects, nurtures, and works for both of you. The Apache blessing that is sometimes read during wedding ceremonies offers the right sentiment—"Now you are two persons, but there is one life before you." But this implies that the "one life" appears—*poof!*—instantly, as soon as you say "I do." In actuality, over the first months and years of your marriage, you and your husband together *create* your one shared life—day by day, discussion by discussion, negotiation by negotiation.

Discovering the personality of your marriage and of yourselves as husband and wife occurs through the small details of everyday life. Maggie Scarf, author of *Intimate Partners: Patterns in Love and Marriage*, describes it as "the marital conversation that moves from bed to breakfast table." During the first year or so of your marriage, you and your husband are in a constant dialogue, working out how you're going to live together as a married couple. As you parse out day-to-day responsibilities, such as who takes care of the car, feeds the dog, and writes the monthly checks, you're building your marriage. As you learn to trust each other with money—"yours," "mine," and "ours"—you're cementing the foundation of your marriage. As you negotiate how much time you spend with family and friends and what aspects of your private life are okay to share, you're co-creating your future together. As you deal with your individual needs for sex and solitude, you're discovering differences you perhaps were not aware of before you married. In short, there's a lot going on inside your cocoon.

Your marriage gains its identity as you develop ways of caring for each other that are unique, ways of living together and loving each other that are private, personal, intimate, and sacred to the two of you. These small acts may not be different from what you did when you were dating—you still have "your" TV show that you enjoy together every Thursday, and you still go out for walks every night after having dinner together—but they're imbued now with a sense of permanence. After making a lifelong commitment, these small activities and gestures, repeated with love and affection again and again, build a sense of family. And often, it's the tiniest details—a loving wake-up routine involving a few minutes of snuggling; or someone receiving a nice hot cup of coffee in bed; or a Post-it note on the dashboard that says "I love you"—that help your family of two develop and flourish.

The process of building an emotionally engaged marriage often begins with play; the goofy games you play together actually make your marriage uniquely intimate and private. Play often gives a marriage part of its personality. When Sarah's under a lot of stress, for example, Jake hides an orange pom-pommed hat in her purse or by the coffeemaker, somewhere he knows she'll find it, laugh, and lighten up. (Then the hat is Sarah's to hide at a later date.) When Alex brings Carrie a plate of cookies, he'll often place one of the favors from her bachelorette party—a suggestive swizzle stick—on top of her stack of Oreos, cracking her up every time. If Cynthia leaves a pair of animal-print underwear on the floor at night, when Brian steps over it, he pretends he's being attacked by a leopard. Would anyone else want to play these games or even think they're funny? Hardly. But these small, silly moments help to build the foundation of your marriage because they're something you and your husband share alone, in the safety, privacy, and intimacy of your marriage, with no one else's awareness.

Developing New Family Traditions

When you create your own family, you have the opportunity to continue the best aspects, traditions, and values from your individual families of origin, and to build upon them. In your first year of marriage, you're starting family traditions that may last a lifetime. Even though Sarah's family is Jewish, they don't embrace many Jewish traditions. But during the first month of her marriage to Jake, she adopted Jake's family ritual of observing Shabbat on Friday nights with a quiet meal at home, just the two of them. Before Shabbat dinner, Sarah lights the Shabbat candles, and Jake drinks from the Kiddush cup. That's the way *they* do things on Friday nights. Soon after Shawna and Mike were married, they started cooking a huge Sunday brunch together. Every week, the menu is exactly the same: waffles, poached eggs, Canadian bacon, and bottomless cups of coffee. They even get out their fancy wedding china. That's the way *they* do things on Sunday mornings. During their first holiday season together, Jasmine and Tim happened to buy their Christmas tree on December 21, the solstice, which is the longest, darkest night of the year. That year, with bottles of wedding champagne still knocking around their apartment, they had lots of bubbly as they lit and decorated their tree, with Bing Crosby and Ella Fitzgerald Christmas carols playing on the stereo. They've continued that simple solstice tradition, because that's the way *they* do things on December 21. Rituals, routines, and traditions all contribute to the intimacy, privacy, and uniqueness of your family.

The Housewife Trap

In the first months of marriage, it's likely you'll jump in headfirst into the role of "wife" without really thinking about how you want to play the role. Instead of going to the gym after work, for example, you may head straight home to play with your new Crock-Pot and Cuisinart, whipping up three-course dinners on a Monday night with grace, ease, and aplomb. To continue the magic of the wedding, you may light candles in your husband's family heirloom candelabra on a Tuesday evening. You may wear the teddies and baby-doll sets from your lingerie shower instead of his boxers to keep things spicy on Thursdays. And you may unwittingly take on most of the household chores, because, you think to yourself, "That's what a 'good wife' does." But before you know it, you've become someone you don't quite recognize: the perfect housewife.

"I feel like I've become this woman from the nineteen fifties, cooking and cleaning and taking care of my husband," said Gillian, who had the low-key wedding by the creek (preceded by Pepto-Bismol). "But that's not who I am or what I signed up for when I got married! I don't want to live like that, and I don't have time to scrub the toilets every week. Nor do I want to, but there's something inside of me that says it's my job, not Rick's—even though Rick has never asked me, specifically, to do these things. So I put on my rubber gloves, scrub the toilets, and resent him as I'm doing it. I feel like I've gotten into a vicious cycle of being a wife and resenting that I'm a wife at the same time."

Gillian's problem isn't at all unusual. I get calls all the time from newlyweds who are confused about what it means to be a wife, and who are having trouble interpreting the role in a way that works for them. In my experience, in their eagerness to be a "good wife," many newly wedded women grab hold of the first image of "wife" that comes to mind, and that's "house-wife." June Cleaver. Donna Reed. Carol Brady (minus Alice, the maid). Our TV culture has embedded into our psyches outdated images of what it means to be a "good wife," ideals created decades ago by most male TV writers. Still, many newly wedded women use this scrub-the-tub ideal of a house-wife as a temporary scaffold while they build their own image of what it means to be a wife within themselves. In their zeal to be a "good wife," they overly embrace the fifties TV image, despite the fact that they are twenty-first-century, educated women who spend most of their time at the office.

And they hate it. After a few months of cooking and clean-ing (while still holding down their jobs, of course), they stand at the coffeemaker brewing the hubby his coffee, and they think, "What the hell am I doing?"

Driving to work the day of her epiphany, Gillian vowed she would shed the housewifely attitude she'd adopted and reclaim her own identity. After three months of living in blissful newlywed la-la land (the good part of being newly married) and another three months being a perfectionistic housewife (the bad part), she yearned to reconnect with her-self as an individual. That week, she threw herself into her work and made a point of staying at the office late many nights, leaving Rick to fend for himself for dinner. (No can-delabra this week, buddy!) She rejoined her book group, and on Friday night she went out to a bar with her single girl-friends. She spent Saturday night at her parents' house, with-out Rick, and made plans to go away for a girls' weekend with her best friend later that month.

Revisiting her old life, however, didn't solve the problem. "I made myself busy, busy, busy, and didn't see much of Rick, and that didn't feel right," Gillian told me. "I missed him, and I didn't like leading such separate lives." Six months into her marriage, Gillian felt like she didn't fit into either her married or her single world. Like many women in the first months of marriage, Gillian's identity was still in flux, and she swung from one extreme of identity—being a housewife—to the other—going back to life as a single girl. Neither end of the spectrum felt quite right.

Spending time in her prewedding life wasn't a waste, however. Out at a nightclub with the girls or at her parents' house without Rick, Gillian discovered that she had already changed after just six months in the cocoon of marriage. Her relationship with Rick had, in that brief amount of time, become her top priority and the new organizing force in her life. She felt more deeply bonded to him—much more than she had before the wedding. And without him intimately involved and participating in the tiny details of her everyday life, Gillian felt like something was missing. Already, she had become one-half of an interdependent married couple. That's how she knew she was growing into her role as a wife.

Not all newly wedded women channel June Cleaver the way Gillian did, but in my experience, most do battle with that false ideal at some point during their first year of marriage. Cynthia and Brian (of the black leather, shabby-chic couch fame), for example, both had demanding jobs; she was a creative director at an advertising agency and he was a lawyer on the fast and grueling track to partner. One night, they were out at a restaurant with another couple and began sharing their tales of newlywed life.

"Do you guys get to have dinner together most nights?" asked their friend.

"Cynthia's great with dinner," Brian replied. "She makes fabulous reservations at restaurants."

"Hey!" Cynthia said. "What do you expect? I'm at work until eight, just like you. Do you really think I'm going to go to the grocery on the drive home, put on an apron, and whip up chicken cordon bleu for you? Come on!"

"No, no, that's not what I mean," Brian said, backpedaling. "I'm just joking. Jeez, can't you take a joke?"

Usually, Cynthia can, but not when she felt like Brian was commenting on the way she had taken on the role of wife. The rest of the evening, she felt angry at him for making the joke, especially in front of this other couple. In their case, the wife had a low-key job and was an excellent cook, and the husband was constantly being told how lucky he was to have married her. But Cynthia also felt mad at herself for second-guessing how she was performing the role of wife, because she thought she was doing a good job at what was really important: tending the marriage, not Brian's tummy.

"As you might expect, we fought in the cab going home," Cynthia told me. "I totally attacked Brian, saying, 'If you wanted someone barefoot, pregnant, and in the kitchen, you married the wrong woman!'"

"Honey, slow down," Brian replied. "It really was just a joke, and I'm sorry I made it. I don't want you running home every night to make dinner for us. That's crazy."

"Are you sure?" Cynthia asked. She hated that she was feeling insecure, but his comment had rattled her, a reflection of how fragile a newly married woman's attachment to her identity as a wife can be. Cynthia's role hadn't changed much after the wedding, and she was pleased that she hadn't buckled under the internal pressure she put on herself to play the role of housewife. But hearing Brian's comment about her skills at making reservations instead of home-cooked meals had aroused her latent insecurities.

"You know I admire how hard you work," he said. "And I love how successful you are. Come on, hon. You know this."

"I can cook, you know," she said, defensively. "When I have the time. When I'm not traveling on business. When I don't have a million things to do at work —"

"Cynthia!" Brian interrupted. "Stop!"

"Okay, okay," she said. "But can you see how hard it is to withstand all the pressure to be a cooking and cleaning wife?"

"Honey, the maid comes once a week," the ever-practical Brian said.

"I know," she said.

For the first year of their marriage, the internal skirmishes between who Cynthia really was — a twenty-first-century executive — and the housewife ideal continued inside her. Each time Cynthia pressured herself to be more housewifely or got down on herself for not cooking or cleaning as much as she thought she "should," she reacted by diving deeper into her work. At least at the office, Cynthia knew exactly how to play her role.

In Cynthia's case, the pendulum swung even further in the

"work" position. She was so reluctant to fall into the housewife trap that their home life became emptier and more sterile than it had ever been when they were dating. She stopped going to the grocery store altogether. Mold collected on leftover take-out food in the fridge. Dust bunnies gathered in corners where there'd been none before. Their house was a wreck.

Eventually, Cynthia realized that in shunning all aspects of being a housewife, she was missing out on some of its smaller pleasures of nurturing herself, her husband, and her home life, such as having a few basics in the fridge so she could whip up a dinner, changing the sheets on the bed with greater frequency, and watering the houseplants. So she started to pick and choose ways to play the role that felt right. For her, that simply meant making their bed every morning; having cereal, milk, and coffee in the house (no more separate breakfasts on the run); and cooking one dinner on the weekend. Did she fire the maid? Hell no!

Once she dismissed her self-imposed guilt about not playing the housewife role, she arrived at a place where she could define for herself what it meant to be a wife. For Cynthia, that meant nurturing her husband in ways other than making food and cleaning house — through caring and compassion, for example, as well as through her interest in his career and her unwavering support of his dreams. It also meant learning how to be nurtured by him; their marriage was not a one-way street.

For Cynthia, being a "good wife" wasn't about the pots, pans, and mops; it was about being true to herself and expressing her love for her husband in ways that felt authentic to her, that reflected her personality. The more she stayed connected to herself, the more she was able to get comfortable as a wife.

Unfinished Business

Part of the emotional work of the first year of marriage is completing the bridging process that you started during your engagement. It's in the first year of marriage that you finish crossing over the bridge into your new identity as wife.

When she wasn't playing the part of Susie Homemaker and resenting her husband for it, Gillian's marriage to Rick had already enhanced the day-to-day quality of her life, making it richer, fuller, and happier. In the intimacy of their marriage and with him by her side, she felt emotionally steadier and stronger than she ever had. She was happy—with herself, with him, and with their relationship.

The joy in her personal life increased her confidence at work. With Rick as a cheerleader and supporter, Gillian went after a higher-paying, more prestigious job with one of her company's competitors, and after two months of intensive interviewing, she was offered the position. She got the job based on her own skills and expertise, of course, but she readily admitted that having Rick as a steadying presence in her life made the process not only more possible but more pleasant. Gillian had no idea that marriage would affect her career so positively—as long as she put down the mop and broom, that is, and hired a cleaning service instead. "As I went through the whole interview process, I saw how Rick provided me with a safe, nurturing haven so that I could really survive the cutthroat job competition," she told me. "Since we started dating, I've always had him to fall back on, but I feel and trust his presence much more now that we're married."

Out at bars with her single girlfriends, the culture clash between Gillian's new, married life and her old, single life was particularly severe. "That's just not the atmosphere I want to be in anymore, staying out late with guys hitting on me," she told me. "But that's what our little group does: we go out. Since I don't want to do that anymore, though, I feel kind of at a loss about how to spend time with my friends." For the first ten months of her marriage, Gillian pushed herself to go out with the girls. When that became uncomfortable for her, she invited them over for dinner. Having Rick at the table changed the dynamic, however; it wasn't quite the same with him there. Finally, after putting a lot of thought into the situation, Gillian stumbled upon a solution that was simple but perfect—going on long walks and hikes with her single friends on Saturday afternoons, while Rick watched sports on TV, or on weeknights, when Rick was traveling for business.

It took Gillian a long time to reach this solution because changing the routine with her friends—going on a walk instead of going to bars—required her to acknowledge and accept that her relationships with them had changed. She knew she couldn't lose her girlfriends just because she was married. They were her sounding boards, her respite from coupledom, her pals; they were an essential part of her life. So that she didn't lose them, she had to redefine her friendships with her single girlfriends, and after a year of marriage she found a way to do that.

It was with her family of origin, however, that Gillian truly discovered how much she had been changed by her marriage to Rick and how successfully she had completed the work of bridging into her new identity. Twelve months after their wedding, Gillian and Rick began house-hunting. Rick was an architect, and he had very specific ideas about what type of home he wanted. Mostly he wanted a house they could move right into, since he spent his workweeks remodeling and designing his clients' homes. The last thing he wanted for his own home was a fixer-upper.

Gillian's parents, however, who were giving them some money for a down payment, thought a fixer-upper would be a better investment for the newlyweds. Naturally, this created some tension. Before the wedding, Gillian would have tried hard to get her parents to understand the ins and outs of why a fixer-upper wasn't right for them. She would have spent hours convincing them that what she and Rick were doing was right.

Twelve months after the wedding, however, she didn't feel so compelled to have them understand what she and Rick needed. In one year of marriage, Gillian's family loyalties had shifted. "When Rick and I were dating, my loyalties were divided between him and my parents," she told me. "But now, Rick's my top priority. His needs—our needs as a couple— are more important to me than my parents' needs. And while that may sound harsh, and while it's upsetting that they think we're making a mistake by not buying a fixer-upper, there's no question in my mind that siding with Rick is what's best for me, for him, and for our marriage."

After their wedding, Gillian and Rick didn't become only legally married. They became emotionally and psychologically married as well, and they became each other's first and foremost family members. The moment she said "I do," and over the course of her first year of marriage, Gillian's family map changed from this:

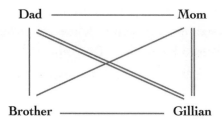

to this:

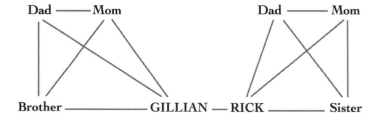

In Gillian's new family map, her healthy, mutually supportive relationship (represented by the single line) with her husband, Rick, is front and center. No longer is Gillian overly close, enmeshed, or entwined with her parents. (Notice that the double line in the first family map has been replaced by the single line, representing a healthier, more balanced relationship.) In the bridging stage, Gillian successfully left her primary family identity of "daughter" so that she could fully embrace her new family with Rick and her new family identity of "wife."

It's a psychological shift that Gillian had begun during the ending stage of getting married and that continued throughout her first year of marriage. She felt the full effect of her shift in family identity during the house-hunting conflicts with her parents. Now a wife and partner who put her and her husband's needs first, Gillian was torn, of course, and it was hard on her to be so misunderstood by her parents, but she knew in her heart that what she and Rick wanted trumped her parents' desires for them.

"In just twelve months, our marriage has become my new North Star," Gillian told me. "I am now orienting my life around it. Not only does that make me a 'good wife,' by my definition at least, but also, this is the type of marriage I wanted. I wanted to be Rick's top priority, and to be that, I've had to put him at the top of my list, too."

Getting to this place of clarity was not without its bumps. Indeed, all newlyweds struggle not only to find their identities as husband and wife, but also to redefine their roles in their parents' families. It's not an easy transition to make, and it's difficult to have divided loyalties and to be confused about what your role is. But it's normal, and it takes time and awareness to work out. Remember: you're in a process. You're adopting your new identity as wife and finding your way in that life. You're in the process of putting your husband and your new family first, and your parents' family second. Be gentle and patient with yourself as you muddle your way through to a newfound sense of balance, with more emphasis on your role as wife.

The Emotional To-Do List Item #15
Your New Family Map

 In your journal, draw your new family map. Place your family with your husband in the forefront, and put your parents' families off to the sides, like this:

Your Parents' Family   Your Husband's Family

You and Your Husband

Mark the emotional relationships in your new family map. Note healthy, emotionally balanced relationships with a single line (I), overly close relationships with a double line (II), rocky relationships with a jagged line (vvv), and cut-off relationships with a broken line (- - - -).

How do you feel when you look at your new family map, which reflects the psychological changes you've been through with your marriage? Along with joy and excitement about the beginning of your new family, it's common to feel sadness, fear, guilt, anger, and anxiety about leaving your family of origin. Reflect on your new and old families and the feelings that come up.

Stage Three

BEGINNING

CHAPTER 10

The New You

Your Life as a Wife

For Better, for Worse

As you now well know, getting married doesn't just happen on your big day. Leaving your single life and becoming a married woman is a process that takes years to fully complete. The journey from the popped question to feeling settled in your married life is a marathon, not a sprint.

Bells won't ring and sirens won't go off indicating that your life as a wife has fully begun. The final stage of your transition from single to married—what I refer to as the "beginning" stage of the Ending, Bridging, and Beginning (EBB) process—is more subtle than that. No longer are you in the throes of your identity change. No longer are you divided between your single and married lives. No longer are your loyalties split between your parents and your husband. Because after eighteen months or so of marriage, your sense of self will once again stabilize.

One way you'll know that you've arrived in your life as a wife is that the questions you worked over in your mind again and again before you got married—"Who am I now?" "What family do I belong in?" and "What kind of wife do I want to be?"—have stopped plaguing you. You will be living and participating in your life as a married woman, not reflecting on it and worrying about it. Your life with your husband will be integrated. You will have evolved from two independent beings to an interdependent couple.

During the beginning stage, it's not so much a question of what you *do*; your job is simply to notice and acknowledge the changes in your sense of identity that have already taken place within you, and to enjoy the new life you are living. So sit back, relax, and read the following stories of some of the women you've gotten to know well in this book as they discover that their transformations from single to married women are complete.

For Richer, for Poorer

By doing the hard work of being emotionally engaged, you learn important skills for marriage—how to let go of old roles and old attitudes, how to allow for change, and how to evolve into a new state of being. You will use these skills as you and your husband continue to grow as individuals within your marriage.

Money had always been tricky territory for Carrie to navigate with Alex. As you may remember, she threw a fit when she heard about Alex's nine-thousand-dollar credit-card debt when they went to apply for a mortgage. After that experience, even though she wanted her life to be as integrated with

Alex's as possible, Carrie was wary about combining finances and reluctant to open a joint checking account. She didn't quite trust that Alex wouldn't go in the hole again. So the couple divvied up the household bills and traded off buying dinner for each other.

Throughout the first few months of their marriage, Carrie kept a running tab in her mind, an account of who spent what. "But about a year into our marriage, I realized that I was spending a lot of time and effort keeping this mental ledger," she said. "Plus, I kept picking fights with Alex whenever I felt like I was the bigger spender. I didn't like how rigid I was becoming about money."

Alex, on the other hand, was far more laid-back about how the couple handled their money. Since he and Carrie made about the same amount, in his mind, whatever he made was hers to spend, and vice versa. He knew they were careful with money (and he had learned his lesson about credit-card debt the hard way, of course, ringing up the charges right after he graduated from college), but he didn't feel the need to keep a penny-by-penny tally.

Alex's mind-set was one that Carrie admired and wanted to adopt. "His approach seemed more loving than my tit-for-tat attitude," she told me. "The more I experienced how he trusted me with money, the more my own rigid attitude started to dissolve."

Six months later, Alex was running late to meet his friends for golf, and he didn't have time to go to the ATM.

"Honey, do you have any money?" Alex asked her, frantically.

"I have lots of cash in my purse," she replied. "Take what you need."

As Alex raced out the door, golf clubs crashing together in his bag, Carrie took note of what had happened: her money didn't feel like *hers* anymore; her money was *their* money. In fact, that incident caused Carrie to reflect that she hadn't been keeping a running tally for the last few weeks. She'd just stopped keeping track. "It didn't matter whose pocket or account it came out of," she told me, "because it was all family money."

Carrie knew that they'd still have many more conversations about money, and they'd still have to make many big financial decisions throughout their marriage, but her newly developed sense of interdependence made the thought of these talks less threatening. She'd come a long way since the days when she'd flipped out about the credit-card balance and kept a running tab of how much she spent. Now, her life was commingled with Alex's. Her attitude about money was just a symbol of the psychological transformation she'd gone through since her engagement.

In Sickness and in Health

Getting through tough times with your husband can also solidify your sense of family and your feeling of being a wife. In fact, many married women tell me that helping their husbands through health crises or going through a death in either of their families bonded them more deeply. Facing life-and-death situations together can often glue newly married couples together more than fun and games can.

Before their wedding, Sarah (the Sociologist) and Jake thought they wanted to start having kids right away. After the wedding, however, when they both realized how precious, intimate, and fleeting their first few months of marriage were, they decided to wait until they were ready. They thought it was important to give themselves time to adjust to all the psychological and emotional changes they'd been through. Plus, they wanted to extend their romantic, intimate life as husband and wife (sans kids) for a little longer.

As their first anniversary approached, they decided to pitch birth control aside. Trying to have a baby initiated a whole new round of questions: How would a baby affect their work? Their identities as individuals? Their lives? Their marriage? But when Sarah used a home pregnancy test to confirm she was pregnant, all their ambivalence quickly shifted into giddiness.

Sarah and Jake kept the news to themselves for, oh, approximately one hour. "We're pregnant!" they announced to family and friends in a flurry of happy phone calls.

At their first doctor's appointment, however, the doctor couldn't hear the baby's heartbeat; Sarah had miscarried.

Sarah sobbed the entire drive home, oblivious to the looks of passengers in other cars. Sadness shook her to the core; she was far more attached to the baby inside of her than she'd consciously known, and her tears would not stop. Jake held it together until they walked through their apartment door.

Then, his jacket still on, he leaned his head on the wall and let out sobs and cries like she'd never heard from him before. Sarah's heart broke in three ways: for their baby, whom they would never know; for herself, whose first experience with motherhood ended in death; and for her husband, who was in inconsolable pain.

Sarah felt powerless. Nothing she said could take away Jake's sadness, just as nothing he said soothed hers. They both knew that the only way to get over the grief was to go through it. And they did. As they grieved, they took turns consoling each other: when one broke down in sobs and in heartache, the other was the soother, the strength, the rock. When one was weak, the other was strong. For days, Sarah and Jake held each other and cried about their lost baby.

The following weeks were a dark period for them as they experienced the breadth of raw emotion: sadness that they'd lost their baby; guilt that they might have done something to cause the miscarriage; anger at the injustice and incomprehensibility of it all. They didn't shy away from their feelings because they trusted them. By facing the emotions as they were happening—by letting them flow through, as Sarah had learned to do when she was stuffing her wedding invitations into envelopes and throughout her engagement—they knew that they would eventually be able to move on.

As grueling as grieving the miscarriage was for Sarah and Jake, sharing the experience of losing their baby and then walking through the grief together knitted them more tightly into a "we." Through the miscarriage, they discovered how they deal with health crises and emotional crises together, and were pleased to discover that they dealt with the crisis they faced really well, in a way that made them both feel cared for and safe. They developed their unique ways of getting through the toughest of times. It solidified the way they do things in their family. Ironically, losing their baby made Sarah and Jake more like a family. For Sarah, holding her husband as he sobbed in pain made her feel more like a wife.

In the sad period that followed the miscarriage, Sarah also sought comfort from her family of origin. It was intolerable for them to see her in so much pain. They all wanted to soothe her, to make her feel better, to make her pain go away. Her parents encouraged her to distract herself from the grief ("Why don't you and Jake take a trip to Europe?"). Her brother urged her to see the reality of the situation ("If that baby had survived, it would have been so sick") or to look ahead to the future ("Why don't you just think about the next baby?"). While their intentions were good, their suggestions didn't help. In fact, their focus on distraction and controlled rationality just made Sarah angry and her pain even greater. Within her family of origin, Sarah felt isolated, alienated, and alone. She didn't fit in with their ways anymore; they were no longer the ones who could provide her with the comfort and support she needed.

The family she did fit into was her family with Jake. In eighteen months of marriage, they had quietly, without conscious knowledge, established their family values, their family behavior, and their family's attitude and approach to life. It differed greatly from her parents' family, but the contrast hadn't become clear until the miscarriage, when the two attitudes toward grief clashed and collided. In the family Sarah and Jake had created, they didn't distract themselves with plans for European vacations; they trusted that their grief was normal and necessary to process. Painful as it was, Sarah discovered through the miscarriage that her allegiance and loyalty had shifted to Jake. With him, she felt emotionally at home. The miscarriage was a watershed event in her growth as a wife, the experience that helped her become aware that she was now comfortable in her own skin as a married woman.

When Sarah got pregnant again three months after the miscarriage, the couple felt truly alone on their path toward parenthood—alone in a good way. Only they understood how scary it felt to be pregnant again, how every little twinge and symptom made them anxious. "Every doctor's visit, test, and ultrasound was stressful because we were afraid we might miscarry again," Sarah told me. "Actually, it was kind of like being a bride all over again: everyone needed us to be *only* happy about this second pregnancy. But only Jake and I could really understand each other's feelings, and that brought us even closer."

The miscarriage and second pregnancy cemented Sarah and Jake's relationship into a union of compassion and understanding. They'd been through so much together, just the two of them, and their challenges served to create a solid foundation for their family. When little Lucy arrived—in perfect health—Sarah and Jake fell immediately, fully, deeply, and head over heels in love with their little girl. "When we were in the hospital, our hearts cracked wide open and let

Lucy in," Sarah said. "It was a major lovefest. The second night, we missed her so much that we padded down to the nursery to visit her at three in the morning! And as we both fell in love with her, Jake and I felt ourselves drop down into an even deeper place of love for each other. It was incredible."

Sarah had traveled a long way since her engagement, when she was focused on problems with her engagement ring and worries about her marriage's effect on her career. In a three-year period, she'd evolved from thinking of herself as *just* a sociologist to, now, a wife, a mother, *and* a sociologist. Her evolution was slow, but it was solid. Sarah felt fully engaged and present in her life with Jake and Lucy.

To Love and to Cherish

As a single woman, Rachel, who had the identity crisis in the yogurt aisle and a tough transition letting go of her dad during her engagement, had loved going on vacations with her parents. She knew it was a little weird, but they enjoyed one another's company, plain and simple. After her wedding to Dave, he started joining the threesome on their trips. His presence added a lot—how great it was to be away with him anywhere!—but it tore Rachel up as well. Whenever they went away as a foursome, her loyalties were divided between wanting to spend time with her husband and wanting to be back in the good old days of just her and her parents together on a trip. Dave tended to be a bit of a slug on vacation and preferred relaxing poolside at the hotel. Her parents, on the other hand, were big sightseers and museumgoers; every moment of their vacations was scheduled and action-packed. Where did that leave Rachel? Darting between Dave and her parents. Going on a vacation as a foursome was highly stressful for her.

When a trip to Paris conflicted with Dave's work, he encouraged Rachel to go without him. "I know how hard it is to constantly ping-pong between your parents and me," he said. "I think you should go and just focus on being with them without worrying about how I'm doing. I think it'll be great for you all."

Being in Paris with her parents was in fact familiar and comfortable, like the trips she'd taken with them before she was married. They went to the Louvre not once but twice (Dave never would have had the patience for that!). They strolled backstreets and poked in and out of shops. They lingered over meals in boisterous bistros. "I loved being in Paris with my parents," Rachel told me. "After so many trips of feeling pulled between my family identities of 'wife' and 'daughter,' it was kind of relaxing to play only one role. My loyalties weren't divided one bit."

But she felt that something was missing as she played the role of daughter. It didn't seem to fit anymore. Having done the grief work during her engagement, she no longer connected to that old identity anymore, and she found herself missing Dave terribly. To dull her longing for him, she made mental notes of things they'd enjoy doing together on a return trip—places they'd go, restaurants they'd try. Being without him also prompted an important insight for Rachel.

"Central though my parents are and always will be in my life, in Paris, I realized that *Dave* is my family now," she explained. "He's the person I feel most at home with. He's the one I feel safest with. He's the one who nurtures me the most, and whom I nurture most. He's the one with whom I share my life. He's my top priority. He's everything to me."

During the first year of her marriage, Rachel had slowly but surely oriented her life around Dave, but she hadn't noticed the extent of it until she spent an entire week *just* as a daughter. It was then that she realized how far she'd come, that she had arrived in her married life, and that she was happy to be there. "Being away from him helped me to see that during the previous year, I had made a real shift in family identity. I wasn't aware of it while it was happening, but it became really clear on that trip."

For as Long as You Both Shall Live

Distance does make the heart grow fonder, especially for couples who've been married a few years. It does so by providing time and the right atmosphere to reflect on your life. For Cynthia, who had gotten engaged amid the bears in Alaska, all it took was one night on her own to gain a different perspective on how far she'd come from her single days, and how much richer and happier her life had become.

Brian was traveling on a business trip the night of a friend's big birthday bash, so Cynthia went solo. "I had a ball," she told me. "I felt like I was single again." Cynthia hadn't felt that free and unattached since before she'd married Brian two years earlier. Slipping back into her old, familiar ways, she worked the room, bopping from person to person, meeting new people, running into old friends, and playfully but innocently flirting with handsome strangers. She even encountered a few flings and some old flames from her single days.

Seeing old boyfriends from across the room caused Cynthia to feel a charge she hadn't felt in years. She had no complaints about her sex life with Brian, but it was, after a time, comfortable, consistent, and familiar. The price of all that comfort? The initial erotic *zing* that she remembered from dating the guys who were at the party. When she talked to her old beaux, though, the loin-tingling stopped. After just a few minutes' conversation, her excitement was replaced by gratitude — gratitude that she didn't end up with any of them, and gratitude for the guy she *did* marry.

As she drove home from the party, Cynthia reflected on how much she valued the marriage she and Brian had created. In previous relationships, Cynthia had always bailed at the first sign of turbulence. But with Brian, she got back into the ring to wrestle things out and find a way to make their marriage work. Together, they'd fumbled their way through the first year, butting heads about who makes the bed and how much time they spend with her parents, among a host of other things.

Individually, Cynthia had struggled to let go of her tight grip on the *Jerry Maguire* theory of marriage: the idea that your spouse should "complete you." In the early months, Cynthia had looked to Brian to be the only source of her happiness. She was no longer particularly satisfied with her career, and she had lost touch with most of her close friends, who were still living a single lifestyle that revolved around dating, parties, and group ski trips. So she looked to her marriage to fill those holes, to complete her. "Bad idea," Cynthia told me. "I eventually learned that my individual happiness is my responsibility, not his. If I moan and groan at dinner every night about my job, there's not much Brian can do but listen. It's up to me to make most aspects of my life as fulfilling as I can. And when I do that, I'm a better partner, a better wife."

It was a tough lesson, but Cynthia learned the necessary balance between independence and interdependence. Two years into their marriage, Cynthia was engaged in a new job, had reconnected with some of her single friends, and had developed new relationships with other women through her work and some volunteer activities she got involved in. She was once again content with her life and proud of the person she was, and she felt that she could bring a lot and give a lot to Brian and their marriage—especially when Brian started experiencing some setbacks in his career and in his confidence. Now it was Cynthia's turn to support Brian. As he struggled through the tough times, she showed him the same patience and love that he had shown her in the early days of their marriage. Cynthia was glad to return the favor, glad that she was in a strong place where she could take care of him.

In a way, Cynthia epitomizes the experience of women who have done the hard work of being emotionally engaged. She was able to make the transition from the woman who was afraid of being devoured by marriage (symbolized by that bear outside the tent) to someone who could find a new kind of strength within her marriage. The way Cynthia puts it speaks, perhaps, for all emotionally engaged women: "I've learned that despite what's happening to Brian and me individually, our marriage is a constant," Cynthia said. "It's like there are three aspects to our marriage: there's me, there's Brian, and there's our marriage itself. Whether we're up or down as individuals, our marriage is this solid, safe, steadying force in our lives. Our marriage is a haven from the storms of life, as well as a place for joy and play and fun. As we grow and change individually, so does our marriage. It's a living, evolving, changing entity unto itself. It's bigger than the two of us as individuals."

As a bride-to-be, busy grieving your single life while checking off items on your to-do list, this last statement about your marriage one day becoming bigger than the two of you may seem a long way off. And it should be. The psychological transition from single woman to married woman that you're going through is a slow evolution, one that occurs in three gradual stages. If you can take each stage step by step, let yourself feel whatever emotions you feel, and be gentle with yourself, you'll be doing all that you can to build a strong foundation for your marriage — one that will be able to thrive for as long as you both shall live.

BIBLIOGRAPHY

Bowen, Murray. *Family Therapy in Clinical Practice*. New York: Jason Aronson, 1978.

Bradshaw, John. *Bradshaw On: Healing the Shame That Binds You*. Deerfield Beach, FL: Health Communications, 1988.

———. *Bradshaw On: The Family*. Deerfield Beach, FL: Health Communications, 1996.

Carey, Benedict. "Watching New Love as It Sears the Brain," *The New York Times*, May 31, 2005, p. D1.

Chassman, Deborah, and Catherine Jhee, eds. *Here Lies My Heart: Essays on Why We Marry, Why We Don't, and What We Find There*. Boston: Beacon Press, 1999.

Cohen, Kate. *A Walk Down the Aisle: Notes on a Modern Wedding*. New York: W. W. Norton, 2001.

Eliade, Mircea. *Rites and Symbols of Initiation: The Mysteries of Birth and Rebirth*. New York: Harper & Row, 1958.

Fielding, Helen. *Bridget Jones's Diary*. New York: Viking, 1998.

Finnamore, Suzanne. *Otherwise Engaged*. New York: Knopf, 1999.

Gottman, John, with Nan Silver. *The Seven Principles for Making Marriage Work: A Practical Guide from the Country's Foremost Relationship Expert*. New York: Three Rivers Press, 1999.

Greer, Jane. *Adult Sibling Rivalry: Understanding the Legacy of Childhood*. New York: Crown, 1992.

Guerin, Philip J. Jr., et al. *The Evaluation and Treatment of Marital Conflict: A Four-Stage Approach*. New York: Basic Books, 1987.

Heen, Sheila. "What Not to Worry About," *Real Simple*, September 2004, pp. 293–94.

Hendrix, Harville. *Getting the Love You Want: A Guide for Couples*. New York: HarperPerennial, 1988.

Heyn, Dalma. *Marriage Shock: The Transformation of Women into Wives*. New York: Villard, 1997.

Kingston, Anne. *The Meaning of Wife*. New York: Farrar, Straus and Giroux, 2004.

Kübler-Ross, Elisabeth. *On Death and Dying*. New York: Scribner Classics, 1997.

Lee, Jenny. *I Do. I Did. Now What?! Life After the Wedding Dress*. New York: Workman, 2003.

Leonard, Linda Schierse. *On the Way to the Wedding: Transforming the Love Relationship*. Boston: Shambhala, 1987.

Levinson, Daniel J. *The Seasons of a Woman's Life*. New York: Borzoi Books/Knopf, 1996.

McDonough, Yona Zeldis, with Howard Yahm. *Tying the Knot: A Couple's Guide to Emotional Well-Being from Engagement to the Wedding Day*. New York: Penguin, 1990.

Metrick, Sydney Barbara. *I Do: A Guide to Creating Your Own Unique Wedding Ceremony*. Berkeley, CA: Celestial Arts, 1992.

Munro, Eleanor, ed. *Wedding Readings: Centuries of Writing and Rituals on Love and Marriage*. New York: Penguin, 1989.

Murdock, Maureen. *The Heroine's Journey Workbook*. Boston: Shambhala, 1998.

Napier, Augustus, with Carl Whitaker. *The Family Crucible: The*

Intense Experience of Family Therapy. New York: Harper-Perennial, 1978.

Nichols, Michael P., and Richard C. Schwartz. *Family Therapy: Concepts and Methods*. Boston: Allyn & Bacon, 1998.

Paul, Sheryl. *The Conscious Bride: Women Unveil Their True Feelings About Getting Hitched*. Oakland, CA: New Harbinger, 2000.

Ragland, Gar, and Meg Ragland with Louisa Kasdon. "I Do. (Now What?)," *The Boston Globe Magazine*, February 13, 2005, pp. 18–23, 31–33.

Roiphe, Anne. *Married: A Fine Predicament*. New York: Basic Books, 2002.

Safier, Rachel, with Wendy Roberts, LICSW. *There Goes the Bride: Making Up Your Mind, Calling It Off, and Moving On*. San Francisco: Jossey-Bass, 2003.

Satir, Virginia. *Peoplemaking*. Palo Alto, CA: Science and Behavior Books, 1972.

———. *Satir Model: Family Therapy and Beyond*. Palo Alto, CA: Science and Behavior Books, 1991.

Scarf, Maggie. *Intimate Partners: Patterns in Love and Marriage*. New York: Random House, 1987.

Stark, Marg. *What No One Tells the Bride: Surviving the Wedding, Sex After the Honeymoon*. New York: Hyperion, 1998.

Stone, Betty S. *Happily Ever After: Making the Transition from Getting Married to Being Married*. New York: Doubleday, 1997.

U.S. Census Bureau. *Statistical Abstract of the United States: 2004–2005: The National Data Book*. Washington, DC: U.S. Government Printing Office, 2004, p. 88.

van Gennep, Arnold. *The Rites of Passage*. Chicago: University of Chicago Press, 1960.

Wallerstein, Judith S., and Sandra Blakeslee. *The Good Marriage: How and Why Love Lasts*. New York: Houghton Mifflin, 1995.

ACKNOWLEDGMENTS

First and foremost, I'd like to thank all the brides-to-be with whom I've worked both individually and in workshops over the years. Your stories are the backbone of this book, and your willingness to work through and grow from your "unbridely" feelings will inspire future brides-to-be to do the same. It's been an honor to walk down the bridal path with you. To the women I interviewed for this book, thank you for sharing your personal journeys from fiancée to wife with such generosity.

Many people have helped in the writing of this book, and I'm grateful for each and every one. Many thanks to Elisabeth Weed of Kneerim & Williams, my agent, cheerleader, and friend. To Laureen Rowland, my editor/publisher, and Danielle Friedman, assistant editor, at Hudson Street Press, for pushing me to find just the right voice and for your thorough line edits; both of you are savvy, speedy, and smart! To those who read and commented on my manuscript in its various incarnations: Susan Blake, Betsy Cunningham, Laura Donahue, Julie Moir Messervy, Carla Zilbersmith, and especially Kristen von Summer Waldorf. To Jamie Kershaw, for kicking me into gear; to Catherine Bradford, for shaping my book proposal; and to my wedding-industry colleagues: Dawn McGrath of maweddingguide.com, BethAnn Schacht, and the members of the Boston Wedding Group. To three very important women: Ceil Berlin, for your compassion and gentleness; Maureen Murdock, for your early support of this idea; and Mary Turner, for your deep and loving friendship. To my parents, William G. and Alice Moir, for giving me the wedding of my dreams. Mom: if we hadn't squabbled about the lasagna, this book would not exist, so thanks. Finally, to my family: my daughter, Annabel, who was born between the writing of the first and second drafts, for being such an easy-going, sweet-tempered baby during this intense time. You've been a grounding presence. And to my husband, Jason E. Smith, for taking such good care of our girl while I worked, and for supporting me every word of the way. Every single day, I'm grateful for you. ILBL. Thank you, my darlings.

ABOUT THE AUTHOR

Allison **Moir-Smith, MA,** is a psychotherapist who specializes in counseling brides-to-be and founded Emotionally Engaged Counseling for Brides in 2002. An expert on cold feet and engagement anxiety, she has appeared on *Today* and *Good Morning America* and has been featured in *Cosmopolitan*, *Elegant Wedding*, and *Elle*. Allison has a master's degree in counseling psychology from Pacifica Graduate Institute and a bachelor's degree from Dartmouth College. She lives in Brookline, Massachusetts, with her husband and daughter.

For information about her bridal counseling services (in person or on the phone) and workshops for brides-to-be, visit her Web site at www.emotionallyengaged.com.